The Tragedy of Romeo and Juliet

Editors:

MAYNARD MACK
Sterling Professor of English, Yale University

ROBERT W. BOYNTON
Former Principal, Senior High School,
and Chairman, English Department, Germantown Friends School

Other editions available in this series:

The Tragedy of Hamlet
The Tragedy of Macbeth
The Tragedy of Julius Caesar
The Tragedy of Romeo and Juliet

THE TRAGEDY OF ROMEO AND JULIET

by William Shakespeare

Edited by

Maynard Mack and Robert W. Boynton

BOYNTON/COOK PUBLISHERS
HEINEMANN
PORTSMOUTH, NH

Boynton/Cook Publishers, Inc.
A subsidiary of Reed Elsevier Inc.
361 Hanover Street
Portsmouth, NH 03801
Offices and agents throughout the world

ISBN 0-86709-035-9

Printed in the United States of America

06 05 04 DA 11 12 13 14

PREFACE

The Mack-Boynton editions of Shakespeare offer the plays most widely studied in schools and colleges, in a format designed to be read more easily than the normal pocket-sized editions, yet inexpensive, durable, and, more important, informed by the best in modern Shakespeare scholarship. The plays included in this series are judiciously framed with supporting material, enabling the reader to deal creatively with the text in the classroom, in small groups, or independently.

The editors of this series have founded their work on the following principles:

(1) Reading Shakespeare is not a poor substitute for seeing Shakespeare well performed, but rather a different arena of experience with its own demands and rewards.
(2) Seeing and hearing the language of the play in the theater of the mind is central to the experience the playwright provides.
(3) Knowing something of the characteristics of Shakespeare's own theater lessens the danger of asking the wrong questions about the structure and meaning of his plays.
(4) The text should be as faithful as possible to the most authoritative early edition, with a minimum of editorial interpolation.
(5) Notes and glosses should explain and not simply suggest, but at the same time readers should be granted their common sense and mother wit.
(6) Commentary before and after the play does not detract from direct experience—is not intrusive—if it suggests ways of approaching the text that allow the reader a broader range of imaginative involvement.

(7) Questions on the text provoke further questions and provide deepened insight if they are not used or thought of as prodding or testing devices.

Each volume in the series contains an introductory essay which briefly puts the play in its historical context (not because our interest is in theatrical history, but because the play *has* a historical context) and discusses the play's themes and concerns and how Shakespeare went about dramatizing them. Along with the introductory essay is a brief note about the Elizabethan theater, a conjectural reconstruction of the Globe Playhouse, and a general note on the policy of this series with respect to texts, with specific reference to the play in hand.

Included in the material following the text are questions, specific and general, on the play, some brief information about Shakespeare himself, and a chronological listing of his works.

CONTENTS

INTRODUCTION

i

Like many of Shakespeare's plays, *Romeo and Juliet* owes much of its continuing popularity to its variety. In mood and plot a tragic work, presenting with a rare sympathy the ecstatic passion of two very young lovers doomed by a combination of impetuousness, bad luck, and the total incomprehension of hostility all around them, it obviously offers at the same time many of the attractions of high comedy. The characters are individualized, it is true, well beyond the usual comic types; but they show nonetheless some recognizable blood-ties with the kinds of people we expect to meet with in stage and film comedy: the Beautiful Ingenue, the Convention-Ridden Parents including the Irascible Father, the Parent-Approved Suitor, the Dashing Romantic Suitor, the Male Confidant and Female Confidante, the Bumbling Well-Meaning Counselor, and the rest.

In the great majority of its scenes, moreover, the play keeps firmly before us a detached comic perspective on events whose tragic intensities we are simultaneously being asked to share. This is the case for nearly all the lovers' scenes, where our sympathy for their rapture or peril is likely to be qualified by a certain amusement at their total self-absorption. It is also true of the two scenes, frequently misunderstood by critics though rarely by audiences, in which the lovers respond, successively, with embarrassingly exaggerated rhetoric, to the new circumstance of Tybalt's death and Romeo's banishment (III ii–iii). No rhetoric that Shakespeare meant us to take seriously would have been accompanied, we may be sure, by (in Juliet's case) the hilarious obbligato of the Nurse as she tries to escalate to the upper registers of romantic grief—"Ah, weraday! he's dead, he's dead, he's dead!" (III ii 38)—or (in Romeo's case) by the irrelevant relevancies of the Friar. The Friar's fussy moralism as he flutters about the prone body of his hysterical charge, trying with wise saws and edifying examples to poultice a wound inaccessible to any verbal comforts, let alone these, is as laughable in its way as the adolescent antics that call it forth. Audiences sense this instinctively. Though their hearts may go out to the lovers in their helplessness, they laugh at everyone concerned—and they should. No one knew better than the author of *A Midsummer Night's Dream* (written either just before or just after *Romeo and Juliet*) that young love, even in anguish, can be extremely funny as well as, on occasion, breathtakingly beautiful.

Even more complicated feelings arise during the Capulets' mourning for Juliet (IV v). On the one hand, our knowledge that they are not bereaved in fact makes for a detachment in our attitudes that is only increased by the comic fluency, not to mention the imaginative barrenness, of their grief: "But one, poor one, one poor and loving child"—"O day, O day, O day, O hateful day!"—O love! O life! Not life, but love in death!" On the other hand, we can hardly help compassionating in some degree a sense of loss that we know is real for *them,* and this compassion is inevitably deepened by what we sense or know they have in store. Comic now, this grief ironically looks forward to the tragic grief to come. Such episodes create a tragicomic texture for the play in which fooling is almost as much at home as feeling, and in which each way of looking at the world casts light upon the other.

Yet more important than these comic elements in the play's total effect is its incorporation of romance—meaning by romance the conventions and value systems of popular romantic fiction. The very fact that the tragedy depicted is a tragedy of lovers must have emphasized for its first audiences that its deepest roots lay in romance, not tragedy; for true tragedy, Elizabethan pundits never tired of declaring, must deal with graver matters than love—with the fall of princes or the errors and sufferings of actual historical men and women in high place. Shakespeare's venture in conceiving *Romeo and Juliet* as a tragedy was therefore in some degree an innovation, possibly an experiment. Instead of personages on whom the fate of nations depended, it took for its hero and heroine a boy and girl in love; and instead of events accredited by history, its incidents were culled from the familiar props of the romantic tall tale: deadly feuds, masked balls, love-at-first-sight, meetings and partings by moonlight and dawn, surreptitious weddings, rope-ladders, sleeping potions, poisons, reunions in the grave—an intoxicating mix!

Furthermore, having decided to make young love his theme, Shakespeare went all the way. His only source—a long narrative poem by Arthur Brooke called *The Tragicall Historye of Romeus and Juliet* (1562)—had used its romantic yarn to carry a sober moral. "To this ende (good Reader)", Brooke tells us in his preface, "is this tragicall matter written":

> to describe unto thee a coople of unfortunate lovers, thralling themselves to unhonest desire, neglecting the authoritie and advise of parents and frendes, conferring [i.e. keeping] their principall counsels with dronken gossyppes [like the Nurse], and superstitious friers (the naturally fitte instrumentes of unchastitie) [Brooke shows marked hostility throughout his poem to the institutions of Roman Catholicism], attemptyng all adventures of peryll, for th' attaynyng of their wicked lust, usyng auricular [i.e. aural] confession (the key of whoredome, and treason) for furtherance of theyr purpose, abusyng the honorable name of lawefull mariage to cloke the shame of stolne contracts, [and] finallye, by all means of unhonest lyfe, hastyng to most unhappye death.

In the poem itself, Brooke shows more sympathy with his young lovers than this prefatory warning would lead us to expect; but, for all that, their affair remains in his telling largely what it had been in several earlier tellings in Italian prose: a pathetic but commonplace attachment, memorable mainly for the sensational incidents and bizarre ironies of mischance with which it is entwined. Only in Shakespeare's hands did the lovestory itself become the lyrical celebration of youthful passion that we all associate with the names of Romeo and Juliet today.

ii

Certainly, nowhere in literature has such passion been more winningly—and more flatteringly—portrayed. Juliet is given by her creator, besides beauty, a loving woman's selfless devotion together with a child's directness, and both qualities remain undimmed to the end:

> My bounty is as boundless as the sea,
> My love as deep. (II ii 138–39)
>
> O churl! drunk all, and left no friendly drop
> To help me after? (V iii 168–69)

Romeo, though much more self-conscious than she, is provided with an energy of imagination that, once he has met Juliet, a genuine high passion kindles into bursts of adoration that no one who has been in love easily forgets:

> O, she doth teach the torches to burn bright!
> It seems she hangs upon the cheek of night
> As a rich jewel in an Ethiop's ear— (I v 45–47)
>
> Do thou but close our hands with holy words,
> Then love-devouring death do what he dare. (II vi 6–7)
>
> O my love! my wife!
> Death, that hath sucked the honey of thy breath,
> Hath had no power yet upon thy beauty.
> Thou art not conquered. Beauty's ensign yet
> Is crimson in thy lips and in thy cheeks,
> And death's pale flag is not advancèd there. (V iii 91–96)

The transforming effects of love are further evidenced in the fact that it brings both lovers whatever personal maturity their short lives allow them to attain. Under its strong direction, Juliet advances swiftly from the little-girl naiveté of her first responses to the idea of marriage ("It is an honor that I dream not of": I iii 68) through deceptions and stratagems and thence to her cry of physical longing as she waits for the horses of the sun to bring night and night to bring Romeo: "Gallop apace, you fiery-footed steeds" (III ii 1 ff). From there it is yet another giant step to the choice that her resolution to remain "an unstained wife to my sweet love" (IV i 89) requires of her, yet she makes it without an instant's hesitation or regret: "If all else fail, myself have power to die" (III v 253).

Romeo, who has further to go than she, begins more derivatively. His love-melancholy at the play's opening is obviously in some part a pose. It evidently gives him pleasure to see himself in the role of Disappointed Suitor, Victim of a Cruel Cruel Maid, and he accordingly acts out for his friend Benvolio most of the attitudes that in his time were supposed to accompany that role—sleeplessness, avoidance of company, lassitude, despair—not forgetting the voguish language of antitheses, paradoxes, and strained metaphors that he voices in his first explosion about the feud and his frustrated love for Rosaline:

> Why then O brawling love, O loving hate,
> O anything, of nothing first created!
> O heavy lightness, serious vanity,
> Misshapen chaos of well-seeming forms,
> Feather of lead, bright smoke, cold fire, sick health,
> Still-waking sleep, that is not what it is! (I i 174–79)

What Shakespeare shows us in such speeches is a young man more interested in parading his symptoms than in the cure of his disease.

Thanks, however, to the feelings set aglow in him by Juliet, all this changes. From preoccupation with his symptoms, he rises to raptures that are real even if excessively self-conscious in the so-called first balcony scene ("How silver-sweet sound lovers' tongues by night," II ii 173), and later to the tenderly insistent realism of his replies to Juliet during the second balcony scene:

> Night's candles are burnt out, and jocund day
> Stands tiptoe on the misty mountain-tops. (III v 9–10)

Now it is she, not he, who longs to linger in the flattering dream: "Yond light is not daylight; I know it, I" (III v 12).

Then follows his lonely encounter with the apothecary: "I sell thee poison; thou hast sold me none" (V i 86). This, more than any other episode, seems to mark symbolically Romeo's coming of age. Its function in the play is much like that of similar encounters in folktale and romance where the hero shows his worthiness by attaching value to some unprepossessing gift or secret obtained from a sinister old man or woman. Certainly Romeo's emphatic rejection here of gold—not only, as he puts it, "poison to men's souls" (V i 83), but an appropriate emblem of all the materialists in the play who would make love serve their ends—constitutes his ultimate accreditation as a romantic hero. This is only confirmed by his recognition that poison is for him "cordial and not poison" (V i 88) since by its means he will "lie . . . tonight" with Juliet in senses earlier unimagined.

Though Shakespeare allows to neither of his protagonists in this play the full tragic realization of what has happened to them that he will allow such later figures as Hamlet and Othello, much less any anguished questionings about their own contribution to it, both do eventually reach a maturity of feeling, if not of understanding, that was not theirs at the play's beginning.

Of climactic significance in this exaltation of romantic love is the fact that the lovers are permitted to maintain, in the face of all the influences that might corrupt or compromise it, an absolute integrity of devotion to each other, and to express it with a lyricism untouched by the playful cynicism or teasing sexual badinage so often indulged by Shakespeare's lovers elsewhere. That the play has been unfailingly popular through so many centuries onstage (as well as, nowadays, in several film versions) may be traced in some part to this fact. Audiences respond to this love-story as to an exemplum, a model, an ideal. And though the vision it delineates has about as much resemblance to our ordinary human gropings in these areas as the Aphrodite of Praxiteles to the efforts of a pottery class, the effect is all the more ingratiating on that account. "Here"—we can tell ourselves, knowing full well that we doubt as we tell it—"is young love realized in its full delicacy, the slim bright edge of the new moon: here is what the experience of first love ought to be, can be, at rare moments has been—for others if not for us: *vivat Eros!*"

iii

Around this idealized love-affair Shakespeare sets swirling a host of competing ideas, giving each its own idiom. Sampson and Gregory, for instance, with their crude talk of maidenheads, weapons, pretty pieces of flesh and the like, announce a cluster of attitudes in which love appears mainly as a form of male aggressiveness: "I will push Montague's men from the wall and thrust his maids to the wall" (I i 15–17). Soon after this, when the noise of the street-brawl (verbal aggression having exploded into physical aggression) subsides, we hear Romeo and Benvolio discussing the inaccessibility of Rosaline. Here we have the other side of the coin—not male aggression but female coquetry carried to the point of tyranny and in its pride rejecting not simply Romeo's advances but all advances: "She hath forsworn to love" (I i 224).

The idiom now is Petrarchan—drawn, that is to say, from a tradition of images and poetic conventions that goes back ultimately to the poems addressed by the Italian poet Petrarch to a woman named Laura, whom (for what reasons is not clear) he was content to worship from afar. Over the centuries, it had become a standard literary love-language, used most often, as in Petrarch's case, to explore and express the emotions involved in a lover's longing for an unattainable beloved—whether unattainable because indifferent (like Rosaline in the play), or simply sequestered from the company of young men (as Elizabethan girls normally were till married), or already bespoke in marriage (as Juliet would have been had Romeo met her for the first time a week later). Longing being its chief subject-matter, much of the vocabulary of this tradition featured love as a perpetual, forever unavailing amorous warfare, with Venus as patron of the battle, Cupid as archer, and the beloved as unconquerable stronghold or invulnerable foe. This is the imagery that Romeo and Benvolio resort to in describing Rosaline as one who goes "in strong proof of chastity well armed" and "will not stay the siege of loving terms" (I i 211–13). It is also the imagery that Mercutio parodies whenever he and Romeo meet.

In this conversation, as noticed earlier, we are introduced to Romeo's own affectations, and then, as if to complete a sequence from "brutal" (Sampson and Gregory) to "coquettish" (Rosaline) to "faddish" (Romeo) to "conventional," we turn to Paris and old Capulet. The young wooer, as Elizabethan protocol dictated, approaches the young lady's father with a proposition. The father predictably replies (with an apparent unconcern that soon fades): Why hurry?—Still, it's all right with *me* if you can obtain *her* consent (I ii 1–19). Predictably also, the mother visits the daughter and dwells upon the attractions of the suitor, especially on how fitting it will be for a Capulet to be the binding that locks in so much wealth:

> That book in many's eyes doth share the glory,
> That in gold clasps locks in the golden story. (I iii 93–94)

No nonsense about love's embraces here: only gold clasps.

Meantime, to these materialist attitudes, the Nurse plays shrill echo. One of Shakespeare's most brilliant early character sketches, she is a shrewd but garrulous, warmhearted but naively vulgar soul, who finds it impossible to answer a simple question without dredging up with it all the seaweed that clings about it in her memory. The question is only about Juliet's age, but by the time the Nurse has settled it she has included her dead daughter Susan, an earthquake, Juliet's weaning, an absence of the elder Capulets in Mantua, and a vulgar witticism of her dead husband's about Juliet's falling and bumping her head. The unfading pleasure she takes in this little sexual joke (not to mention the kind of comparison that springs instantly to her mind when she describes the size of Juliet's bump) tells us most of what we need to know about *her* understanding of romantic love. After hearing her on the subject of "falling backward," we are not likely to be much surprised by her response to the proposal for Juliet's marriage: "Go, girl, seek happy nights to happy days" (1 iii 108). Or by her response later to Juliet's agony, when, being already married to Romeo, she faces a second forced marriage to Paris:

> Beshrew my very heart,
> I think you are happy in this second match, [lucky]
> For it excels your first; or if it did not,
> Your first is dead—or 'twere as good he were
> As living here and you no use of him. (III v 232–36)

This contrast between the Nurse and Juliet is reinforced by Mercutio's contrast with Romeo. Mercutio knows all about the supposed pangs that love occasions and can speak that language as well as Romeo:

> You are a lover. Borrow Cupid's wings
> And soar with them above a common bond. (I iv 17–18)

But he speaks it only to mock it. Knowing well that such feeling is often self-deceived—a disguise, in fact, for simple appetite—he appears to cherish the conviction that such it must always be: all that is real is sex. To every protest that Romeo makes about the preoccupations of his heart, Mercutio replies with a bawdy quip. He knows all about Queen Mab, too, and can describe her equipage with childlike wonder, enchantingly—until again he mocks her: he has no serious interest in what she represents. Our psychic inner-world of fancy, longing, mystery, and dream (on which Juliet will later confer a cosmic rhythm and splendor by associating it with the chariot of the sun god Apollo: III ii 1 ff), Mercutio here dismisses and shrinks to insignificance by associating it with the minuscule chariot of Mab, in whose Skinnerian world we are all reduced to programmed stimulus and reponse:

> And in this state she gallops night by night
> Through lovers' brains, and then they dream of love;
> O'er courtiers' knees, that dream on curtsies straight;
> O'er lawyers' fingers, that straight dream on fees;

O'er ladies' lips, who straight on kisses dream . . .
(I iv 74–78)

On the same "rational" grounds, Mercutio refuses credence to Romeo's dream and his consequent misgivings about going to the Capulet feast.

The play is to prove him wrong on several of these points, and the first instance occurs at once. For the "conjuration" of Rosaline that Shakespeare puts into his mouth as he and Benvolio look for their vanished companion after the ball (II i 8 ff) places this washroom chatter in immediate juxtaposition with the luminous beauty of Juliet and the exalted feelings she has stirred in Romeo—both of which we have just witnessed. Useful as an antidote to the maudlin worship of the Beautiful Cruel Lady (La Belle Dame sans Merci) whose caprices have enslaved Romeo, Mercutio's witty pruriencies are now seen to have come up against something to which they are irrelevant. Irrelevant, most obviously, because directed at the wrong girl. But more deeply irrelevant, too, because so determinedly excluding the capability that men and women have of valuing each other as persons rather than sexual objects and of placing that value above all other imaginable values—exactly what we have just seen taking place a few moments earlier as Romeo and Juliet stand isolated from the rest of the world in the fourteen lines of a love-sonnet.

The rapt unanimity of feeling that they share within that sonnet unfolds, as the play proceeds, into the radiant experience that the coarser attitudes we have just been examining help to define and set apart. To earn our belief in that experience, or at the very least a suspension of our disbelief, Shakespeare undertakes to validate it for us by showing us that *he* is aware of crasser possibilities, even if his lovers are not; that he knows what he shows us in them is not within the reach of all—not, for instance, the County Parises of the world, however admirable they may be for other virtues; that he knows, even where it exists, such love as this is always under threat, not only from those whose values are determined by convention, like the Capulets, and no doubt equally the Montagues, but from those, like Mercutio, whose appraisal of human capabilities it considerably transcends, and from those, like the Nurse, with whose jovial but crude sensibility it is quite out of tune; and, moreover—a sufficiently tragic concession in itself—that he knows it must in the long run face defeat—if not by the world, then by our mortal nature, which allows nothing to remain in perpetuity, or even for very long, the thing it was. Everything that grows, he laments repeatedly in his Sonnets, "Holds in perfection but a little moment." In some part, *Romeo and Juliet* seems a poignant elaboration of that thought, in dramatic terms.

iv

Just here, the play *may* intend to raise questions as well as paeans around the romantic experience it so much exalts. What, for instance, do the repeated hints that this love is as dangerous as it is beautiful—perhaps beautiful *because* dangerous—signify? Like the blaze of gunpowder, says Friar Laurence:

> These violent delights have violent ends
> And in their triumph die, like fire and powder,
> Which, as they kiss, consume. (II vi 9–11)

To be sure, the friar is an old man, skeptical of youth's ways; yet can we help reflecting on this diagnosis when we recall at the play's end that five young people have died: Mercutio, Tybalt, Paris, Romeo, Juliet? Does it suffice to hold the feud alone accountable?

Then there is the repeated situation of enclosure. With the exception of their marriage scene at the exact center of the play, we see Romeo and Juliet together only in the interval between evening and dawn, and always in a kind of enclave or special space which is threatened from without. At the ball, they are framed by a sonnet and by a sudden quiet that is made the more striking and precarious by Tybalt's attempted intrusion. In the first balcony scene, their enclosure is the Capulets' walled garden, and the interview is twice on the point of interruption by the Nurse. In the second such scene, whose setting is Juliet's chamber, their leavetaking *is* interrupted, first by the Nurse's warning and then by Lady Capulet's appearance. Even in the tomb, the social order intervenes, in the person of the Friar, between Romeo's suicide and Juliet's.

Plainly, in some degree, what goes on here, apart from the requirements of the plot, is a playwright's rendering of the feeling of intense but vulnerable privacy that all lovers know. "To be in their state of mind," says a recent critic, "is to be in a world of one's own. . . . The contrast between the world of the lovers and the world of other people is itself a universal feature of the experience of being in love, and the plot of the play gives a dramatic heightening to this universal fact by placing this love in the midst of a feud between the lovers' families. . . ." So much the play clearly tells us. Does it also tell us that the unreconcilability of this love with the ordinary world is a tragic consequence of its nature, a trait not separable from it without destroying the thing it is—and so more tragic on that account?

Similar ambiguities hover about the relationship established between the passion of Romeo and Juliet and the death that seems to be implicit in it. Significantly, the last scene takes place in a tomb. This is a remarkable dénouement, and we have been prepared for it by a succession of references, prophetic of the outcome even when dropped casually or in ignorance, in which love and death are identified or closely linked. First, by Juliet herself:

> Come, cords; come, nurse. I'll to my wedding bed;
> And death, not Romeo, take my maidenhead!
> (III ii 139–40)

Soon after, by her mother, angered at her disinclination to marry Paris: "I would the fool were married to her grave" (III v 144). Next, by her father, supposing that his daughter's apparent death on the eve of her wedding is real: "Death is my son-in-law, Death is my heir" (IV v 41). Later, by Paris, acting on the same supposition at the tomb: "Sweet flower, with flowers thy bridal bed I strew" (V iii 12). And finally by Romeo:

> Shall I believe
> That unsubstantial Death is amorous,
> And that the lean abhorrèd monster keeps
> Thee here in dark to be his paramour?
> For fear of that I still will stay with thee. . . . (V iii 102–6)

The playwright's insistence throughout on pairing the bride-bed with the grave reaches a climax in the tomb-scene, where death and sexual consummation become indistinguishable as Romeo "dies" (a word often used in Rennaisance literature to refer to the culmination of the sexual act) upon a kiss, and Juliet, plunging the dagger home, sighs: "there rust, and let me die" (V iii 120, 175).

We must recall, too, that from the moment they acknowledge their love these lovers have been made to sense that it spells or may spell doom:

Is she a Capulet?
O dear account! my life is my foe's debt. (I v 124–25)

If he be marrièd,
My grave is like to be my wedding bed. (I v 141–42)

Their apprehension can be attributed in part to the feud, but only in part. Juliet's lines above are spoken while she is yet in ignorance of Romeo's identity, and Romeo's premonitions of "Some consequence, yet hanging in the stars" (I iv 113) precede even his visit to the ball. We in the audience, moreover, have been assured from the very beginning that this love is "death-marked" (Prologue, 9).

What are we to make of such evidence? Does the play urge us to conclude that every high romantic passion, by its very finality and absoluteness, its inwardness and narcissism, is necessarily allied with death, even perhaps (however unconsciously) seeks death? being oblivious of all competing values to a degree that ordinary human lives cannot afford and determined to hold fast to a perfection that such lives cannot long sustain? and therefore tending irresistibly to a "love-death" because unable or unwilling to absorb the losses imposed by a "love-life"? Or is the implied connection at once simpler and more universal: that death is always the "other pole" required to generate love's meaning—the little negotiable domestic loves that most of us aspire to as much as the austerest romantic pang? that *our* loves, too, are "death-marked" and (in the senses that matter most) "star-crossed," because both marked and crossed by the general human fate, which is to die? and therefore that those audiences are right after all who, despite the play's concern with a particular pair of lovers in a particular situation, sense in it a universal parable that speaks eloquently to their own condition?

v

There are no certain answers to these questions, or even to the question whether the playwright intends them to be asked. What *is* certain is that when we see *Romeo and Juliet* in performance, or perform it alertly for ourselves in the theater of the mind, such problems tend to vanish in an experience that is altogether dramatic: an experience that owes more to gestures, groupings, movements onstage, stunning intensities and reversals of human feeling, breathtaking effects of color, light, and sound, than to theoretical considerations of the sort we have just been examining.

Consider, for instance, the first scene. Two swaggering boneheads in Capulet livery—the livery very probably a little frowsy like their manners and speech, their swagger only making more conspicuous the fear it is meant to hide—meet two similar figures wearing the contrasting colors of the Montagues. A scuffle follows. The stage resounds with cries, grunts, heavy-footed lunges, clumsy whacks and thwacks of short swords on small shields—the habitual armor of the lower classes. Though violent, the scene has at first a comic coloring, thanks to the ineptitude of the contestants, who show a marked disinclination to get hurt. Then, in almost instantaneous counterpoint, comes the encounter of the two young gentlemen. In dress, speech, and physical grace, they are "civilized" to a degree that the household servants are not; but once engaged they are far more deadly, for they fight with rapiers and are animated by a code of honor that stakes life itself on skills of hand and eye.

Thus comic violence draws in tragic violence—a foretaste of much to come—while around the two contending groups a general fracas grows. Some elderly citizens rush in carrying weapons as ancient as themselves and labor, farcically, to quell the fighting. On their heels come old Capulet and Montague, comic figures likewise, since neither their manifest years and frailty nor the supposed wisdom of old age has been able to abate their mindless commitment to the feud. Finally, his entry no doubt announced by a trumpet fanfare, the Prince arrives with his retinue. The authority of the state, expressed now in the regular declamatory rhythms of the Prince's "sentence" (I i 85–99), prevails for the time being over individual passions, and the crowd drifts rapidly away. What we have been shown is the susceptibility of a whole society to be cleft from top to bottom by an inherited vendetta (in our world it could as easily be some other inflexible frame of mind) in which, we soon discover, no one but Tybalt has more than a face-saving interest. Yet thanks to the atmosphere the feud has given rise to, even the peace-making Benvolio—the man of "good will," as his name implies—can be drawn into a street riot against his better judgment, and the security of the entire community can be put in jeopardy on the whim of a determined fool—a Malvolio, or man of "ill will," as Tybalt might equally have been called.

The entrance of Romeo is timed for this moment, following the outbreak rather than before it, to make the encumbrance of the feud, his blood-inheritance, crystal clear. Over the conversation that Benvolio holds with the elder Montagues, which prepares us for Romeo's appearance (alone, distracted, his clothing very possibly disheveled as the clothing of those subject to love-melancholy was popularly supposed to be), and also over the conversation that Benvolio holds with him, the shadow of the violence we have just seen hangs heavily. The condition of "death-marked love," to which the Prologue has called attention (line 9), is thus acted out in a half-comic form that will quickly become tragic. Like Hamlet, who in some ways resembles him, Romeo has inherited a time which is "out of joint" and which nothing short of his own and several other "misadventured piteous overthrows" (Prologue, line 7) can redeem. Still comparatively detached from the feud as we encounter him now (though already "in love" with a Capulet), he will be drawn moment by moment further into its quicksands, each apparent escape—e.g. the marriage with Juliet, which should *unite* the two families—becoming an additional step in the progress of events that sweeps both lovers to their doom.

Here, then, is one way in which *Romeo and Juliet* comes powerfully home to us in performance: as a fast-moving succession of situations, each gripping in itself but also making part of a headlong race to ruin, even though that race does not lack for the little ironical postponements and detours that allow an audience teasing hopes of a happier issue. But the play registers in other emphatic ways as well. As an experience of vivid contrasts, for instance, in a world that is tense with polarities of every sort. Extreme youth—Juliet is only 14, Romeo (we may guess) in late adolescence—tugs at extreme age, for despite Lady Capulet's odd comment at I iii 71–73 all four parents give the impression of being somewhat along in years, as are obviously the Friar and Nurse. Passionate love grapples with passionate hate, and eventually, at great cost enjoys an ambiguous triumph. The brightness of the lovers, in their images of each other, dazzles against the darkness of their situation, while at the same time, paradoxically, the night world becomes more and more their sole resource and the daylight world more and more the possession of forces inimical to them. Then there are the sharply conflicting attitudes toward love and sex, already touched on; the extremes of haste and deliberation; the great joys giving way to overwhelming griefs; the noise, bustle, and uproar of public affairs juxtaposed against the hushed inward-turning ecstasies of lovers' longing and lovers' meeting.

All these opposites and many more make part of our experience in this play, but again not as theoretical contraries—only as vivid impressions of eye and ear. To take one more example, worldliness and innocence—an innocence not yet broken by the world—are among the polarities on which *Romeo and Juliet* is founded, but they take shape onstage only in the particularized form of Juliet, sitting (in I iii) a little apart from her elders, perhaps wearing some white garment in keeping with the impression she seems intended by her words to make on us; while her nurse and mother, each with characteristic motives and pre-occupations, preside over what we recognize as a coming of age, a tribal *rite de passage,* a "debut," in short, into what both older women take to be her appropriate next phase in the human life-cycle of birth, copulation, and death. Eventually, her innocence outwits their wisdom, but the price exacted is appalling.

vi

In conclusion, something must be said about what for many of today's readers and spectators is the most striking single feature of *Romeo and Juliet:* its formalism. The pronounced general symmetries that have gone into its configuration are obvious enough. Three confrontations of the warring houses, each followed by a pronouncement from the Prince, mirror each other successively at I i, III i, and V iii—except that the consequences crescendo in seriousness: no one dies during the first, two are dead after the second, and three, including the protagonists, after the third. Equally visible at a glance are the variations played on balancing personalities: a bawdy Nurse flanks Juliet in I iii and a bawdy Mercutio flanks Romeo in I iv; or, again, a sober Benvolio, trying to cool a hot Tybalt in I i, parallels a sober Benvolio trying to cool a hot Mercutio in III i. Yet, curiously enough, this stress on "forms" only evokes more keenly, when the play is seen and heard, our sense of its immense reserves of dramatic and linguistic power. As a highbred horse shows his truest fire when curbed, so the artifices of the play's style and structure create a condition of containment from which its energies break out with double force: energies that explode on the slightest provocation into horse-play, sword-play, word-play, love-play; energies that smolder in Tybalt's and Lady Capulet's hatred of the Montagues and bubble over in Mercutio's witty scorn of everything that looks like posturing or fakery, whether Romeo's premonitions and dreams (I iv), Tybalt's dancing-masterish fencing style (II iv 20ff), or the Nurse's affectation of being a *grande dame,* all got up in her best fineries with a man-servant to go before (II iv 94–135); energies, furthermore, that flow like a high-voltage current through the love scenes, idealizing everything they touch, and in the potion and tomb scenes so overpower all other considerations that Juliet can drink off the Friar's potion despite her terror, and Romeo can unhesitatingly storm the Capulet tomb in order to be reunited with his wife on their mutual death-and-marriage-bed.

Behind all these energies, of course, releasing but at the same time shaping them, stands the energy of Shakespeare's own imagination, in sheer exuberance of creation melting down old forms to make them new. The ancient conceit comparing the beloved lady's beauty to various kinds of dazzling light becomes in his hands Juliet hanging upon the cheek of night like a rich jewel in an Ethiop's ear (I v 45–47), Juliet showing at her window like a sunrise in the East (II ii 2–3), Juliet making even the grave "a feasting presence full of light" (V iii 86). Similarly the time-worn conception of the lover as a ship tossed by storms of passion or misfortune in the attempt to reach safe harbor in his lady's favor takes on in Shakespeare's reinterpretation of it a passionate urgency:

> I am no pilot; yet, wert thou as far
> As that vast shore washed with the farthest sea,
> I should adventure for such merchandise. (II ii 85–87)

Later, when Romeo swallows the apothecary's drug, this timeworn metaphor is strikingly reinterpreted:

> Come, bitter conduct; come, unsavory guide!
> Thou desperate pilot, now at once run on
> The dashing rocks thy seasick weary bark!
> Here's to my love! [*Drinks.*] O true apothecary!
> Thy drugs are quick. Thus with a kiss I die.
> (V iii 116–20)

So too with the lover's "blazon." Properly speaking, the

blazon in Renaissance love-poetry is a descriptive inventory of the beloved's charms, moving lingeringly and luxuriously, item by item, from her golden hair to her shapely foot. In *Romeo and Juliet,* the convention reappears, but is significantly displaced from the true beloved (Juliet) to the imagined beloved (Rosaline), is subordinated to a formula of conjuration derived from demonology (possibly a further insult), and is spoken not by the lover in praise of the beloved but by the scoffer, who throws doubt on the whole spectrum of high romantic feeling by indicating very clearly what he believes to be its crass sources:

> I conjure thee by Rosaline's bright eyes,
> By her high forehead and her scarlet lip,
> By her fine foot, straight leg, and quivering thigh,
> And the demenses that there adjacent lie,
> That in thy likeness thou appear to us! (II i 19–23)

But these verbal transformations are only the surface outcroppings of Shakespeare's originality in *Romeo and Juliet.* What many in his audiences must have responded to at a deeper level, unanalyzed but felt, is the presence of certain psychological experiences familiar to all who have ever loved, for which he has managed to find in his story of two hapless lovers unobtrusive but unforgettable dramatic forms. One such experience is the mysterious mix in every sexual passion of attraction and repulsion, love and hate. *Odi et amo*: "I hate and I love," wrote the Roman poet Catullus, and Shakespeare has captured the phenomenon memorably in his play, not simply in dramatizing a quite literal mixture of attraction and repulsion in Juliet when her husband kills her kinsman, but in keeping at all times clear the psychological interface between the love story itself and its environment of hate. The very phrases in which contemporary and earlier poets had summed up the latent antagonisms of the sexes as well as the power of a particular beloved woman to hurt her lover by disdain—woman seen as "dearest enemy," an unconquerable "fortress," a warrior with "killing" eyes—become charged with new meaning in *Romeo and Juliet* through their radical implication in the plot itself:

> My only love sprung from my only hate! . . .
> Prodigious birth of love it is to me
> That I must love a loathèd enemy. (I v 145, 147–48)

> Alack, there lies more peril in thine eye

Than twenty of their swords! (II ii 74–75)

Thou are not conquered—Beauty's ensign yet
Is crimson in thy lips and in thy cheeks,
And death's pale flag is not advancèd there. (V iii 94–96)

Similarly with the masculine sense of woman as a mysterious being withheld—a being to be wooed, not conquered, and only to be fully known when given by her own free choice. This sense—a constant theme of Elizabethan love-poetry—pervades the play, and again the favorite images and phrases of the literary tradition take on a new and glowing life through being reinterpreted in action. In his chatter about Rosaline, Romeo had invoked idly the Petrarchan image of woman as unyielding fortress, but when this image returns at the play's end, in the last passage quoted above, the unyielding fortress is plain to be seen on the stage in Juliet's yet living form, and it is only to the paramour death, not Romeo, that she lies unyielding. When Romeo reclaims her for his own by freely choosing to be her husband in death as well as life, she gives herself in turn to be again his wife by her free choice in falling upon his dagger. What is also to be observed is that this same sequence of events has already been acted out in the happier setting of the Capulet garden. To that garden—which is itself partly a dramatic realization of the parallel that from Biblical times had been drawn betwen a virgin and a *hortus conclusus* or closed garden—Romeo is attracted by desire. The girl he meets there, however, though virgin, is so far from being an Unconquerable Fortress or a *Belle Dame sans Merci*, that she can show her love for him more freely and less self-consciously than he can show his for her:

My bounty is as boundless as the sea,
My love as deep; the more I give to thee
The more I have, for both are infinite. (II ii 138–40)

It is no more than appropriate, therefore, that when he ascends to her chamber for their wedding night, it is by means of a rope-ladder that he has supplied and she has lowered to him. The Petrarchan image of woman as fortress, unyielding and therefore to be taken only by assault, yields, like his own experience of Rosaline, to a truer definition to which love is a gift to be freely given and received.

The most remarkable among the ancient phrases that Shakespeare regenerates by causing them to be acted out in front of us is every lover's conviction that love must conquer death: *Amor vincit omnia.* Around this phrase and the corresponding psychological urgencies, the play's last scene is plainly built. Romeo, as has already been pointed out, asserts his claim to Juliet against death's claim; in the person of the Lover he breaks open the Tomb, which by the power of his passion and her beauty is transformed to a feasting presence-chamber filled with light; and though he dies beside her, he manages to carve out through his idealizing imagination an enigmatic space—last of the many enclaves in which we see them—in which death and sexual consummation coincide—"Thus with a kiss I die"; "There rust, and let me die."

vii

An awesome close to a lavish pageant of romantic feeling. Yet we must not suppose that Shakespeare intends us to let it go entirely unchallenged. Against its idealized shape, complete with operatic deaths and high flown lyric utterances, he has already set for our contemplation a far messier, prosier, less predictable death-scene—one much more like those we meet with in our own world: Mercutio's. Mercutio's death is anything but a consummation and far from being lyrical in either content or form. Like his parody of the lover's blazon earlier, his last words seem calculated to puncture and shrivel up yet another body of posturing and pretense—that a man's death is to be reckoned some sort of special or heroic occasion—that it comes about (as in romantic literature generally) only after great deeds, great wounds, or meeting with a great adversary (in fact, even a cat's scratch will do it)—and that it must not by any means be accompanied by expressed resentments or ironies, but only by such noble expressions of magnanimity and acceptance of one's fate as accord with the idea of making a good end.

ROMEO. Courage man, the hurt cannot be much.

MERCUTIO. No, 'tis not so deep as a well, nor so wide as a church door; but 'tis enough, 'twill serve. Ask for me tomorrow and you shall find me a grave man. I am peppered, I warrant, for this world. A plague a both your houses! Zounds, a dog, a rat, a mouse, a cat, to scratch a man to death! A braggart, a rogue, a villain, that fights by

> the book of arithmetic! Why the devil came you between us? I was hurt under your arm. (III i 94–102)

No pithy "last words" here: only scorn and anger at the sheer contingency and arbitrariness of what was quite unnecessary but has nevertheless taken place.

This death and these speeches—indeed all of Mercutio's speeches—suggest a possible other scale in which the lovers' devotion to each other and their "victory" at the close may be weighed. Looked at through *his* perspective, the lovers' ideal experience of each other, the exalted images they feed on, the absolute fidelity to which they sacrifice their lives must be reckoned among the fictions by which men and women deceive themselves about their true natures and the nature of their world. On the other hand, looked at through *their* perspective, his reading of reality must appear near-sighted and reductive, for the fictions men and women live by are the best road they have to truth, whether about themselves or about the world.

In *Romeo and Juliet* Shakespeare has juxtaposed these two divergent value systems—the last and climactic pair of contraries in that scheme of contrasts at which we earlier glanced—without allowing them to touch. Mercutio never learns of Romeo's mature love for Juliet, and his death is well behind us when we encounter theirs. Perhaps the playwright feared that either view, if brought too close to its opposite, would shatter. Later, he will be more venturesome. His tragic heroes from Hamlet on are required to know the world in both perspectives simultaneously and the experience tears them apart, as it still does some of us today:

> What a piece of work is a man, how noble in reason,
> how infinite in faculties; in form and moving how
> express and admirable, in action how like an angel,
> in apprehension how like a god: the beauty of the
> world, the paragon of animals; and yet to me what
> is this quintessence of dust? Man delights not me;
> nor woman neither. . . . (*Hamlet* II ii 309–15)

A Note on the Elizabethan Theater

Most present-day productions of Elizabethan plays use sets designed to provide a single flexible and suggestive background against which their multiple scenes can flow easily one into the next. Elizabethan plays have to be staged that way if they are not to be distorted, because that is the way they are built. Though the modern playwright is limited by the nature of his theater to as few changes of locale as possible, his Elizabethan counterpart was encouraged by *his* theater to range the whole world of space and time, because his theater was in fact an image of the world. Shakespeare's own theater was even called the world—i.e. the "Globe."

In today's theaters, for the most part, audience and play are emphatically separate. They are separated physically by the architecture of the theater, which has a drop-curtain, footlights, often an orchestra pit, and always a proscenium arch (the arch covered by the curtain), on one side of which the audience sits hushed in almost total darkness, while on the other side the persons of the play move and talk in spots, or floods, of blazing light.

This physical separation of audience from play is expressive of the figurative gulf which, in our theater, also divides them. For the illusion that the modern theater imposes is that the audience is "not really" present, but is eavesdropping, and that the people it looks in on are "really" men and women going about real business in a real room from which one wall has been removed.

What this means for those on the bright side of the footlights is that everything must be made as completely "present" as actors, scene-painters, and stage-carpenters can manage; it is not enough to suggest reality, it must be simulated. The implication for those on the dark side of the footlights is that they must become as "unpresent" as they can—in other words detached, silent, and passive, like the eavesdroppers they are. Actually, neither of these extremes is ever reached in our theater, or even closely approached, but the tendency of enhanced realism on one side of the curtain to generate passivity on the other has spurred many modern playwrights to search for ways of recapturing the cooperative relation between audience and play that Shakespeare's theater had.

Physically the Globe was a wooden building shaped probably like a polygon outside and circular inside, some thirty or forty feet high, with three tiers of roofed galleries, one on top of the other straight up, opera-house style, around the entire interior. The center of the enclosure (the "pit"), some fifty or so feet in diameter, was unroofed, and into it jutted the raised rectan-

THE GLOBE PLAYHOUSE, 1599-1613

A Conjectural Reconstruction

Key

AA Main entrance
B The Yard
CC Entrances to lowest gallery
D Entrances to staircase and upper galleries
E Corridor serving the different sections of the middle gallery
F Middle gallery (''Twopenny Rooms'')
G ''Gentlemen's Rooms'' or ''Lords' Rooms''
H The stage
J The hanging being put up around the stage
K The ''Hell'' under the stage
L The stage trap, leading down to the ''Hell''
MM Stage doors
N Curtained ''place behind the stage''
O Gallery above the stage, used as required—sometimes by musicians, sometimes by spectators, and often as part of the play
P Backstage area (the tiring-house)
Q Tiring-house door
R Dressing rooms
S Wardrobe and storage
T The hut housing the machine for lowering enthroned gods, etc., to the stage
U The ''Heavens''
W Hoisting the playhouse flag

gular stage, fully half the way across the pit and almost forty feet wide. Above part of the stage, as a cover, supported on pillars, was a sloping roof, called the "Heavens," the ceiling of which was brightly painted with stars and other astronomical figures. Below the stage, reached by trap doors, was "Hell." At the rear wall, doors on either side gave access between the stage and the dressing rooms. Toward the rear of the stage there was an "inner" playing area, probably a sort of alcove (but sometimes misleadingly called the "inner stage"), which could be left opened or curtained. Directly above this was an "upper" playing area (the "upper stage"), which probably took the form of a balcony. Above this was another, smaller balcony for the musicians; for the use of music, in tragedy as well as comedy, was one of the conventions of Elizabethan plays.

What scenery there was in theaters like the Globe took chiefly the form of simple props. There was no artificial lighting of any kind in the theater, which meant that performances were always given by daylight—in the afternoon. The interior of the building was handsomely decorated, and the dress of the actors (males only—boys played the female roles) expensive and resplendent, although there was little concern for what we would call authentic period costuming.

The important thing to bear in mind about the Elizabethan theater is that the stage physically dominated the open area and that the audience literally enveloped the actors and the action. As many as two thousand people might be present. Many stood shoulder to shoulder in the pit, surrounding the chest-high open platform on three sides. Behind them in the tiered galleries, at no place more than forty or fifty feet from the stage, sat hundreds of others on benches. In these circumstances, it was easy for the viewers' sense of involvement in the play, and the actors' sense of involvement with the audience before and behind them, to become more intense than in our theater.

The playwright who writes for such a theater as this cannot shape his play as if the audience were not "there": it is irremovably there, every member of it visible to every other in the broad light coming from the open roof. So he necessarily acknowledges its presence, engages its imagination. He feels free, for example, to give his characters "asides"—speeches spoken wholly or mainly for the benefit of the audience, and which those on stage are not supposed to hear. He also gives his characters "soliloquies"—longer speeches by means of which the leading characters may open heart and mind directly to the audience. Further, since his stage is a bare platform without scenery, he calls repeatedly on the imagination of the audience to flesh out the suggestions of hour, place, weather, or mood that he can only communicate to them through the play's own words.

The dramatist who writes for the theater we have been describing has unparalleled opportunities to make the theater audience do duty as an extension, an overflow, an amplification of the very limited stage-audiences which a small company of actors can muster. When, for instance, Shakespeare's Antony addresses the Roman mob in *Julius Caesar,* in a theater where we of the audience surround him on three sides, the realization comes on us increasingly as he speaks that it is we who fill out that tiny group of listeners onstage into the formidable mob he *seems* to harangue; and when King Harry in *Henry V* exhorts his soldiers—"You noblest English"—to battle bravely against the French, we realize (as Shakespeare's own audiences must have done, and in their case with a sharp quickening of the pulse) that it is *we* who are being addressed: *we* are those "noblest English" who are being implored never to yield.

Interactions like these between play and audience are not impossible in the modern theater, but they were a good deal easier to effect in Shakespeare's. Partly, as we have noticed, because of the close physical proximity of audience to player. Partly, as we have also noticed, because the audience's imagination was implicated in the play by the very austerity of a stage without scenery. And partly because the Elizabethan theater's inheritance from the medieval theater (where the stories acted out were primarily Bible stories and therefore "true" in one sense while remaining "stories" in another sense) encouraged an easy traffic back and forth between what was "real" and what was "play."

As has been mentioned, over part of the stage stretched a ceiling called the "Heavens," and under the stage, reached by trap doors through which witches and other apparitions might rise, lay an area called "Hell." And in front of the theater, in the case of Shakespeare's Globe (if we may believe a plausible tradition), was inscribed the legend: *Totus mundus agit histrionem*—"Everybody is an actor"; or, as Shakespeare himself paraphrased it in *As You Like It,* "All the world's a stage, and all the men and women merely players." Thus the individual actor whom the audience saw on the stage playing Julius Caesar or Hamlet or Macbeth was capable of being translated, at any moment, by the very symbolism of that stage, into an image of Every Man working out his human destiny (as the men and women watching him would also have to work out theirs) between the powers of Hell and Heaven.

It is because the characters of Shakespeare were created for a theater like this that they take special hold of us. They have the intensity that comes from believing that the world is a stage, where we are given only our little hour to work out eternal salvation or damnation: and they have the grandeur that comes from believing that the stage is a world, which reaches out past the actors to the theater audience, past them to the audience we call history, past this to the cosmic audience of land, sea, air, moon, sun, and stars (which Elizabethan heroes do not hesitate to address), and so at last to the audience Hamlet turns to when the appearance of the Ghost makes it unmistakable that there are more things in heaven and earth than are dreamed of in human philosophies: "Angels and ministers of grace defend us!"

Textual Note

Although Shakespeare had no connection with their actual publication, eighteen of his thirty-seven plays were published in various quarto editions before his death in 1616. Not until 1623 were all but one of the plays usually credited to him published in a single volume, now called the First Folio. (A folio is a book made up of sheets folded in half, creating four individual pages per sheet; a quarto is one made up of sheets folded in half and in half again, producing eight pages per sheet.) The First Folio was compiled by two of Shakespeare's actor-colleagues who drew upon the best previous quarto editions of single plays, where available, and on fairly reliable unpublished manuscripts and theater promptbooks. For whatever reason, they omitted from their collection two plays which most scholars today attribute wholly or in part to Shakespeare (*Pericles, Prince of Tyre* and *The Two Noble Kinsmen*) and one play (*Sir Thomas More*) in which it is believed he had a hand.

The policy of this series is to use the earliest sound version of each play—either the Folio text or (if one exists) a good quarto text with collations from the Folio—and a minimum of emendation. In lineation, we follow a similarly conservative policy. Most modern editors space the line fragments, with which two successive speeches often end and begin, as a single pentameter line. A case can be made for this procedure, but after considerable reflection we have abandoned it, because we believe that in these situations the lineation of the original editions more often than not throws interesting light on speaking emphasis, pause, and rhythm, and also eliminates a possible reading distraction. We have everywhere normalized and modernized the spelling and punctuation of the original texts, printed character names in full, and added (inconspicuously) act-scene divisions, following the practice of the Globe edition (1864), to which concordances of Shakespeare refer. All matter placed in brackets in the text, including stage directions, is editorial and does not appear in the original version being used.

The line numbering and the act-scene indicators at the top of each page are for convenient reference. The small degree sign (°) indicates a gloss or footnote at the bottom of the page, keyed by line number. The cue phrase is printed in boldface, the gloss or footnote in roman.

The only authoritative text of *Romeo and Juliet* is found in the second quarto edition of 1599. This is now generally believed to derive from Shakespeare's own manuscript. An earlier pirated quarto of 1597 preserves a garbled and much truncated version of the play, evidently reconstructed from memory by two or three of those who had performed in it—either for the purpose of selling it surreptitiously to a publisher or performing it on the sly outside of London. This text, bad as it is, affords a number of useful stage directions not found in Q2. These we have adopted. We have also adopted at I iv 7–8 two lines found only in Q1, which are generally agreed to be Shakespeare's. These and all other departures from Q2 are signalized in our notes.

THE TRAGEDY OF ROMEO AND JULIET

[*Dramatis Personae*

CHORUS

ESCALUS, Prince of Verona

PARIS, a young count, kinsman to the Prince

MONTAGUE } heads of the opposed Houses
CAPULET }

AN OLD MAN, of the Capulet family

ROMEO, son to Montague

MERCUTIO, kinsman to the Prince, and friend to Romeo

BENVOLIO, nephew to Montague, and friend to Romeo

TYBALT, nephew to Lady Capulet

FRIAR LAURENCE } Franciscans
FRIAR JOHN }

BALTHASAR, servant to Romeo

ABRAM, servant to Montague

SAMPSON } servants to Capulet
GREGORY }

PETER, servant to Juliet's nurse

AN APOTHECARY

THREE MUSICIANS

LADY MONTAGUE, wife to Montague

LADY CAPULET, wife to Capulet

JULIET, daughter to Capulet

NURSE TO JULIET

CITIZENS OF VERONA, GENTLEMEN AND GENTLEWOMEN OF BOTH HOUSES, MASKERS, TORCHBEARERS, PAGES, GUARDS, WATCHMEN, SERVANTS, AND ATTENDANTS.

Scene: Verona, Mantua]

THE TRAGEDY OF ROMEO AND JULIET

The Prologue°

[*Enter*] *Chorus.*

[CHORUS]. Two households, both alike in dignity,°
  In fair Verona, where we lay our scene,
From ancient grudge break to new mutiny,°
  Where civil blood makes civil° hands unclean.
From forth the fatal° loins of these two foes   5
  A pair of star-crossed° lovers take their life;
Whose misadventured° piteous overthrows
  Doth with their death bury their parents' strife.
The fearful passage° of their death-marked love,
  And the continuance of their parents' rage,   10
Which, but° their children's end, naught could remove,
  Is now the two hours' traffic° of our stage;
The which if you with patient ears attend,
What here shall miss,° our toil shall strive to mend.

[*Exit.*]

I Prologue Often in Elizabethan stage practice, less often in Shakespeare's, a prologue-speaker introduces the play's setting, theme, and subject-matter. (For mockery of the practice within the play itself, see Benvolio's comment at I iv 3-10, and for an extremely funny parody of it, *A Midsummer Night's Dream*, V i 112ff.) Here, the Prologue tells his audience that the play's setting lies in Verona, a circumstance calculated to arouse interest, since Italy for English imaginations had always been connected with sultry passions; that the subject-matter is an ancient blood-feud now breaking out again between two powerful families; and that the theme concerns reconciliation of hate by love, though at the price of the lovers' lives. All this is conveyed in the fourteen lines of a sonnet, possibly because this is a form the Prologue's audience would readily have associated with such expressions of high romantic feeling as the story they are about to see enacted.

1 dignity rank

3 mutiny violence

4 civil/civil i.e. citizens'/citizens'

5-7 fatal, star-crossed, misadventured i.e. doomed (by fate, stars, chance)

9 passage course

11 but except

12 traffic business (since they were acted continuously without scene changes or audience intervals, performance time for many Elizabethan plays was approximately two hours)

14 What . . . miss i.e. what there is no room for in a brief prologue

Enter Sampson and Gregory, with swords and bucklers,° of the house of Capulet. I i

SAMPSON. Gregory, on my word, we'll not carry coals.°

GREGORY. No, for then we should be colliers.°

SAMPSON. I mean, an we be in choler,° we'll draw.°

GREGORY. Ay, while you live, draw your neck out of collar.°

SAMPSON. I strike quickly, being moved. 5

GREGORY. But thou art not quickly moved to strike.

SAMPSON. A dog of the house of Montague moves me.

GREGORY. To move is to stir, and to be valiant is to stand.° Therefore, if thou art moved, thou runn'st away.

SAMPSON. A dog of that house shall move me to stand. I will 10 take the wall° of any man or maid of Montague's.

GREGORY. That shows thee a weak slave; for the weakest goes to the wall.°

SAMPSON. 'Tis true; and therefore women, being the weaker vessels,° are ever thrust to the wall.° Therefore I will push 15 Montague's men from the wall and thrust his maids to the wall.

GREGORY. The quarrel is between our masters, and us their men.°

SAMPSON. 'Tis all one. I will show myself a tyrant. When I 20 have fought with the men, I will be cruel° with the maids —I will cut off their heads.

GREGORY. The heads of the maids?

SAMPSON. Ay, the heads of the maids, or their maidenheads. Take it in what sense thou wilt. 25

I i s.d. bucklers small round shields
1 carry coals put up with insult (coal-carrying being the lowest household chore, the phrase was applied to any degrading service)
2 colliers coal dealers (Gregory, who fancies himself a wit, pretends to take Sampson's phrase literally)
3 an . . . choler if we are angered (by any affront from the Montague household)
3 draw i.e. draw sword
4 collar hangman's noose (like *choler*, a pun on *collier*)
8 stand stay (refuse to give ground)
11 take the wall since the preferred place to walk was against the wall and away from the street, which was unpaved and often dumped upon from upper windows, to "take" the wall was insulting, to "give" it, courteous
12-13 goes . . . wall proverbial for "gets pushed around"
14-15 weaker vessels Biblical phrase for women (1 Peter 3:7)
15 thrust . . . wall given the wall (but with sexual overtones in thrust)
19 men (1) servants (2) males (i.e. maids having nothing to do with it)
21 cruel Q4; Q2 has *civil*

GREGORY. They must take it in sense° that feel it.

SAMPSON. Me they shall feel while I am able to stand;° and 'tis known I am a pretty piece of flesh.

GREGORY. 'Tis well thou art not fish;° if thou hadst, thou hadst been poor-John.° Draw thy tool!° Here comes two of the house of Montagues. 30

Enter two other Servingmen [*of the Montagues*].

SAMPSON. My naked weapon is out. Quarrel! I will back thee.

GREGORY. How? turn thy back and run?

SAMPSON. Fear me not.

GREGORY. No, marry.° I fear thee!° 35

SAMPSON. Let us take the law of° our sides; let them begin.

GREGORY. I will frown as I pass by, and let them take it as they list.°

SAMPSON. Nay, as they dare. I will bite my thumb° at them, which is disgrace to them if they bear it. 40

ABRAM. Do you bite your thumb at us, sir?

SAMPSON. I do bite my thumb, sir.

ABRAM. Do you bite your thumb at us, sir?

SAMPSON. [*aside to Gregory*] Is the law of our side if I say ay?

GREGORY [*aside to Sampson*] No. 45

SAMPSON. No, sir, I do not bite my thumb at you, sir; but I bite my thumb, sir.

GREGORY. Do you quarrel, sir?

ABRAM. Quarrel, sir? No, sir.

SAMPSON. But if you do, sir, I am for you. I serve as good a man as you. 50

ABRAM. No better.

SAMPSON. Well, sir.

---

26 take . . . sense i.e. take as sense (i.e. physical sensation) the act or thing that deprives them of virginity
27 stand hold my ground: see 8n (but here with a sexual undermeaning)
29 fish as distinguished from flesh = butcher's meat (as in "fish, flesh, fowl")
30 poor-John hake (cheapest of fish), dried and therefore shriveled
30 tool sword (but with allusion to the sexual sense, as throughout these lines)
35 marry mild oath, "by the Virgin Mary" (= "heaven forbid")
35 I fear thee!. ."*I* fear *thee?*" (with scorn)
36 take . . . of have the law on
38 list please
39 bite my thumb insulting gesture (made by snapping thumbnail against front teeth) with roughly the same meaning as thumbing the nose

Enter Benvolio.

GREGORY. [*aside to Sampson*] Say 'better.' Here comes one of my master's kinsmen. 55

SAMPSON. Yes, better, sir.

ABRAM. You lie.

SAMPSON. Draw, if you be men. Gregory, remember thy swashing° blow. *They fight.*

BENVOLIO. Part, fools! 60
Put up your swords. You know not what you do.

Enter Tybalt.

TYBALT. What, art thou drawn among these heartless hinds?°
Turn thee, Benvolio! look upon thy death.

BENVOLIO. I do but keep the peace. Put up thy sword,
Or manage it to part these men with me. 65

TYBALT. What, drawn, and talk of peace? I hate the word
As I hate hell, all Montagues, and thee.
Have at thee, coward! [*They fight.*]

Enter three or four Citizens with clubs or partisans.

CITIZENS.° Clubs, bills,° and partisans!° Strike! Beat them down!
Down with the Capulets! Down with the Montagues! 70

Enter old Capulet in his gown,° and his Wife.

CAPULET. What noise is this? Give me my long sword, ho!

WIFE. A crutch, a crutch! Why call you for a sword?

Enter old Montague and his Wife.

CAPULET. My sword, I say! Old Montague is come
And flourishes his blade in spite of° me.

MONTAGUE. Thou villain Capulet!—Hold me not, let me go. 75

MONTAGUE'S WIFE. Thou shalt not stir one foot to seek a foe.

58-59 swashing Q4, slashing (Q2's *washing*, though a possible variant form, is dramatically weaker)
62 heartless hinds cowardly servants (pun on *hinds* = female deer and on *hartless* = without a *hart,* i.e. without a male deer to protect them)
69 Citizens we follow Hosley in taking Q2's speech-heading *Offi.* (= officer) to be a compositor's misreading of *Citti.* (= "confused cries" of several Citizens), since (1) to bring in an official here subtracts something from the climax that is to follow at the Prince's entrance, and (2) both lines seem better suited to the style of citizens than to an officer
69 bills, partisans spear-like weapons with an axe-like blade or spike horizontally placed just below the point
70 s.d. gown dressing gown
74 in spite of i.e. to spite

Enter Prince Escalus, with his train.

PRINCE. Rebellious subjects, enemies to peace,
Profaners of this neighbor-stainèd° steel—
Will they not hear? What, ho! you men, you beasts,
That quench the fire of your pernicious rage 80
With purple fountains issuing from your veins!
On pain of torture, from those bloody° hands
Throw your mistempered weapons to the ground
And hear the sentence° of your movèd° prince.
Three civil brawls, bred of an airy° word 85
By thee, old Capulet, and Montague,
Have thrice disturbed the quiet of our streets
And made Verona's ancient citizens
Cast by° their grave beseeming° ornaments
To wield old partisans, in hands as old, 90
Cank'red with peace, to part your cank'red° hate.
If ever you disturb our streets again,
Your lives shall pay the forfeit of the peace.
For this time all the rest depart away.
You, Capulet, shall go along with me; 95
And, Montague, come you this afternoon,
To know our farther pleasure in this case,
To old Freetown, our common judgment place.
Once more, on pain of death, all men depart.
Exeunt [all but Montague, his Wife and Benvolio].

MONTAGUE. Who set this ancient quarrel new abroach?° 100
Speak, nephew, were you by when it began?

BENVOLIO. Here were the servants of your adversary
And yours, close fighting ere I did approach.
I drew to part them. In the instant came
The fiery Tybalt, with his sword prepared; 105
Which, as he breathed defiance to my ears,
He swung about his head and cut the winds,°

---

78 neighbor-stainèd see Prologue, 4n
82 bloody a first indication of the cost that will grow with each confrontation of the houses: see III i, V iii
84 sentence (1) decision (2) penalty
84 movèd irate
85 airy mere breath, i.e. trifling
89 Cast by put off
89 beseeming i.e. appropriate (for old men)
91 Cank'red . . . cank'red rusted . . . rancorous
100 set . . . abroach opened (term used for opening a cask and letting the wine run)
107 He . . . winds a useful clue to the action of Tybalt in the preceding episode (on his offensively "theatrical" fencing, see II iv 19ff)

Who,° nothing hurt withal,° hissed him in scorn.
While we were interchanging thrusts and blows,
Came more and more, and fought on part and part,° 110
Till the Prince came, who parted either part.

MONTAGUE'S WIFE. O, where is Romeo? Saw you him to-day?
Right glad I am he was not at this fray.

BENVOLIO. Madam, an hour before the worshipped sun
Peered forth the golden window of the East, 115
A troubled mind drave me to walk abroad;
Where, underneath the grove of sycamore
That westward rooteth from this city side,
So early walking did I see your son.
Towards him I made, but he was ware° of me° 120
And stole into the covert of the wood.
I, measuring his affections° by my own,
Which then most sought where most might not be found,°
Being one too many by my weary self,
Pursued my humor, not pursuing his,° 125
And gladly shunned who gladly fled from me.

MONTAGUE. Many a morning hath he there been seen,
With tears augmenting the fresh morning's dew,
Adding to clouds more clouds with his deep sighs;
But all so soon as the all-cheering sun 130
Should in the farthest East begin to draw
The shady curtains from Aurora's° bed,
Away from light steals home my heavy° son
And private in his chamber pens himself,
Shuts up his windows,° locks fair daylight out, 135
And makes himself an artificial night.
Black° and portentous must this humor prove
Unless good counsel may the cause remove.

---

108 Who which
108 withal thereby
110 on part and part on either side
120 ware (1) aware (2) wary
120 Towards . . . me shunning others' society was a symptom (either real or affected) of fashionable Elizabethan love-melancholy
122 affections feelings
123 most sought . . . found most wished to be alone
125 Pursued . . . his i.e. followed my mood by not following (to inquire into) his
132 Aurora the dawn
133 heavy melancholy
135 windows shutters
137 Black i.e. dangerous—but also with allusion to the fact that the Greek word for black *(melan)* makes up the first half of the word melancholy, which in turn is the name of one of the four basic humors (blood, phlegm, choler, and melancholy or black choler) supposed in Renaissance medical theory to constitute a person's temperament or disposition

BENVOLIO. My noble uncle, do you know the cause?

MONTAGUE. I neither know it nor can learn of him. 140

BENVOLIO. Have you importuned him by any means?

MONTAGUE. Both by myself and many other friends;
But he, his own affections' counsellor,
Is to himself—I will not say how true—
But to himself so secret and so close,° 145
So far from sounding° and discovery,
As is the bud bit with an envious° worm
Ere he can spread his sweet leaves° to the air
Or dedicate his beauty to the sun.
Could we but learn from whence his sorrows grow, 150
We would as willingly give cure as know.

Enter Romeo.

BENVOLIO. See, where he comes. So please you° step aside,
I'll know his grievance, or be much denied.

MONTAGUE. I would thou wert so happy° by thy stay
To° hear true shrift.° Come, madam, let's away. 155

Exeunt [*Montague and his Wife*].

BENVOLIO. Good morrow,° cousin.

ROMEO. Is the day so young?

BENVOLIO. But new struck nine.

ROMEO. Ay me! sad hours seem long.
Was that my father that went hence so fast? 160

BENOVLIO. It was. What sadness lengthens Romeo's hours?

ROMEO. Not having that which having makes them short.

BENVOLIO. In love?

ROMEO. Out—

BENVOLIO. Of love? 165

ROMEO. Out of her favor where I am in love.

Rosaline

---

145 close i.e. inward
146 from sounding (1) from being probed (as of a wound) (2) from being measured (as of the depth of seas or rivers)
147 envious malignant
148 leaves petals
152 So . . . you if you please
154 wert so happy i.e. might be so lucky
155 To as to
155 shrift confession, explanation
156 morrow morning (hence Romeo's affectation of surprise in 157)

BENVOLIO. Alas that love, so gentle in his view,°
Should be so tyrannous and rough in proof!°

ROMEO. Alas that love, whose view° is muffled still,
Should without eyes see pathways to his will!° 170
Where shall we dine? O me! What fray was here?
Yet tell me not, for I have heard it all.
Here's much to do with hate, but more with love.°
Why then, O brawling love, O loving hate,
O anything, of nothing first created! 175
O heavy lightness, serious vanity,°
Misshapen chaos of well-seeming forms,
Feather of lead, bright smoke, cold fire, sick health,
Still-waking° sleep, that is not what it is!
This love feel I, that feel no love in this.° 180
Dost thou not laugh?

BENVOLIO. No, coz,° I rather weep.

ROMEO. Good heart, at what?

BENVOLIO. At thy good heart's oppression.

ROMEO. Why, such is love's transgression.° 185
Griefs of mine own lie heavy in my breast,
Which thou wilt propagate,° to have it prest
With more of thine. This love that thou hast shown
Doth add more grief to too much of mine own.
Love is a smoke raised with the fume of sighs; 190
Being purged, a fire sparkling in lovers' eyes;°
Being vexed, a sea nourished with lovers' tears.
What is it else? A madness most discreet,°

---

167 view appearance
168 proof experience (with a pun on *proof* = armor)
169 view sight (Cupid is usually represented blindfolded)
170 see . . . will (1) refers to Cupid's finding ways and means, despite his blindness, to make us fall in love? (2) refers to love's undiscouraged effort to win the beloved's sexual favors?
173 Here's . . . love (1) specifically: because he loves Rosaline of the enemy house, whose inaccessibility will only be increased by the new outbreak of the feud; (2) more generally: because love is by its nature a complex of contradictory states (such as he goes on to register in the fashionable Petrarchan paradoxes of 174-79) and includes its extreme opposite—hate
176 vanity triviality
179 Still-waking ever-wakeful
180 this (1) the street fracas just ended? (2) the buffeting by contraries that love causes (since my love is not returned)?
182 coz cousin
185 transgression i.e. over-passing of proper bounds (i.e. by adding to the grief I feel on my own account the grief of knowing that you suffer grief on my behalf: 186-89)
187 propagate increase
191 Being . . . eyes i.e. when the frustration indicated by the sighs are cleared away, love is joyous
193 discreet sane (to be paired with *madness*, as *preserving sweet* with *choking gall*, 194)

All about love

A choking gall,° and a preserving sweet.
Farewell, my coz. 195

BENVOLIO. Soft!° I will go along.
An if° you leave me so, you do me wrong.

ROMEO. Tut! I have left° myself; I am not here;
This is not Romeo, he's some other where.

BENVOLIO. Tell me in sadness,° who is that you love? 200

ROMEO. What, shall I groan° and tell thee?

BENVOLIO. Groan? Why, no; but sadly° tell me who.

ROMEO. Bid a° sick man in sadness° make° his will?
Ah, word° ill urged to one that is so ill!
In sadness, cousin, I do love a woman. 205

BENVOLIO. I aimed so near when I supposed you loved.

ROMEO. A right good markman. And she's fair I love.

BENVOLIO. A right fair° mark, fair coz, is soonest hit.°

ROMEO. Well, in that hit you miss.° She'll not be hit
With Cupid's arrow.° She hath Dian's wit, 210
And, in strong proof° of chastity well armed,
From Love's weak childish° bow she lives unharmed.
She will not stay° the siege° of loving terms,
Nor bide th' encounter of assailing eyes,
Nor ope her lap to saint°-seducing gold.° 215

Rosaline dosen't love back

---

194 gall bitterness
196 Soft i.e. "not so fast"
197 An if both *an if* and *an* = "if" throughout the play
198 left Daniel's emendation of Qq "lost," which seems unmistakenly a compositor's misreading; *left* not only plays wittily on Benvolio's leave ("Leave *you*? I've even left myself") but alludes more sharply than "lost" to the conventional lovers' claim that the real self, or soul, resides with the beloved (as in 199)
200 in sadness seriously
201 groan Romeo chooses to make Benvolio's *in sadness* to mean "in pain"
202 sadly seriously
203 Bid a Q1; Q2 has *A*
203 sadness (1) taken with *man*, sadness = unhappiness; (2) taken with *make*, sadness = seriously, soberly
203 make Q1; Q2 has *makes*
204 word i.e. "sadness"
208 fair bright, visible
208 mark . . . hit (with a sexual overtone)
209 in . . . miss in that smart (and true) reply, you misjudge the situation
210 Cupid's arrow see 208n
210 Dian's wit the wisdom of Diana, goddess of chastity
211 proof armor (see 168)
212 childish (1) ineffectual (2) belonging to a child, i.e. Cupid
213 stay (1) endure (2) wait for
213 siege i.e. the beloved is seen as an unsurrendering stronghold (a Petrarchan commonplace used in this play with great power: see V iii 94-96)
215 saint Petrarchan term for the beloved: see I v 97-114
215 Nor . . . gold the image is of bribing the garrison of a stronghold to surrender, but with further reference to the story of Danaë, who was seduced when Zeus entered her place of confinement in the form of a shower of gold

O, she is rich in beauty; only poor
That, when she dies, with beauty dies her store.°

BENVOLIO. Then she hath sworn that she will still° live chaste?

ROMEO. She hath, and in that sparing makes huge waste;°
For beauty, starved with her severity, 220
Cuts beauty off from all posterity.
She is too fair, too wise, wisely too fair,
To merit bliss° by making me despair.°
She hath forsworn to love, and in that vow°
Do I live dead that live to tell it now. 225

BENVOLIO. Be ruled by me; forget to think of her.

ROMEO. O, teach me how I should forget to think!

BENVOLIO. By giving liberty unto thine eyes.
Examine other beauties.

ROMEO. 'Tis the way 230
To call hers (exquisite°) in question° more.
These happy masks° that kiss fair ladies' brows,
Being black puts us in mind they hide the fair.
He that is strucken blind cannot forget
The precious treasure of his eyesight lost. 235
Show me a mistress that is passing fair,
What doth her beauty serve but as a note
Where I may read who passed that passing fair?°
Farewell. Thou canst not teach me to forget.

BENVOLIO. I'll pay that doctrine,° or else die in debt. *Exeunt.* 240

217 store wealth (i.e. she will leave no children in whom her beauty is perpetuated, a common complaint in Renaissance love poetry: see e.g. Shakespeare's sonnets 1, 3, 4, 11)
218 still always
219 sparing . . . waste i.e. by being niggardly with her wealth she in fact squanders it (with a pun on "waist" that extends the paradox drawn from wealth (niggardly/squandering) with others drawn from diet (sparing, but growing fat) and sexuality (chaste, but visibly pregnant)
223 bliss heaven
222-23 She . . . despair she is too fair-minded, too prudent, prudently too just to win heaven by dooming me to despair (with the usual puns on *fair* = beautiful and *wise* = discerning); Romeo seems to mean that Rosaline's motive in withholding her favors is not her wish to show her power over him but fidelity to her vow of chastity
224 forsworn . . . vow there is paradoxical play here with Rosaline's being at once "faithful" (to her vow) and "forsworn" (to love), as there is in 225 with "living" and being "dead" and in 226-27 with "forget" and "think"
231 exquisite pronounced éxquisíte
231 in question into consideration (but for the audience this also means "into doubt")
232 masks Elizabethan women of quality often wore black half-masks when in public
232-38 These . . . fair as black masks on beautiful women only remind us of the beauty hidden; as the blind man remembers the glories he can no longer see; so any surpassingly lovely mistress you can show me will serve only as a notation (or a gloss on a text) to remind me of the incomparable original—my Rosaline
240 I'll . . . doctrine I'll render you the lesson I owe you

Enter Capulet, County° Paris, and the Clown° [a Servant]. I ii

CAPULET. But Montague is bound° as well as I,
In penalty alike; and 'tis not hard, I think,
For men so old as we to keep the peace.

PARIS. Of honorable reckoning° are you both,
And pity 'tis you lived at odds so long. 5
But now, my lord, what say you to my suit?°

CAPULET. By saying o'er° what I have said before:
My child is yet a stranger in the world,
She hath not seen the change of fourteen years;°
Let two more summers wither in their pride 10
Ere we may think her ripe to be a bride.

PARIS. Younger than she are happy mothers made.

CAPULET. And too soon marred° are those so early made.
Earth hath swallowèd all my hopes° but she;
She is the hopeful lady° of my earth.° 15
But woo her, gentle Paris, get her heart;
My will to her consent is but a part.
And she agree,° within her scope° of choice
Lies my consent and fair according° voice.
This night I hold an old accustomed feast, 20
Whereto I have invited many a guest,
Such as I love; and you among the store,°
One more, most welcome, makes my number more.
At my poor house look to behold this night

I ii s.d. County count
s.d. Clown not a jester but an uneducated person, a yokel
1 bound under bond
4 reckoning reputation
6 my suit my plea (for Juliet's hand)
7 But . . . o'er all I can say is
9 change . . . years i.e. her fourteenth birthday—which seems early for marriage to us but evidently not to Shakespeare, who found Juliet 16 in his source and reduced her age (Miranda in *The Tempest* is under 15 and Marina in *Pericles* is 14)
13 marred i.e. by childbirth
14 hopes children
15 hopeful lady i.e. hope-inspiring heiress
15 my earth (1) my body? (2) my property?
18 agree Q3, Ff; Q2 has *agreed*, which can be read (somewhat clumsily) to mean "she being agreed" instead of "if she agree"
18 scope range
19 according agreeing (but with allusion to a musical sense implicit also in *consent* and *voice*)
22 and . . . store i.e. and if you will join the gathering

Earth-treading stars° that make dark heaven light. 25
Such comfort as do lusty young men feel
When well-apparelled° April on the heel
Of limping Winter treads,° even such delight
Among fresh female° buds shall you this night
Inherit at my house. Hear all, all see, 30
And like her most whose merit most shall be;
Which, on more view of many, mine, being one,
May stand in number, though in reck'ning none.°
Come, go with me. [*to Servant, giving him a paper*] Go, sirrah,° trudge° about
Through fair Verona; find those persons out 35
Whose names are written there, and to them say,
My house and welcome on their pleasure stay.°

Exit [*with Paris*].

SERVANT. Find them out whose names are written here? It is written that the shoemaker should meddle with his yard° and the tailor with his last,° the fisher with his pencil and 40 the painter with his nets;° but I am sent to find those persons whose names are here writ, and can never find what names the writing person hath here writ. I must to the learned. In good time!°

Enter Benvolio and Romeo.

BENVOLIO. Tut, man, one fire burns out another's burning;° 45
One pain is less'ned by another's° anguish;
Turn giddy, and be holp° by backward turning;
One desperate grief cures with another's languish.°

---

25 stars i.e. girls
27 well-apparelled i.e. in leaves and flowers
28 treads the image is of a dance figure in which limping Winter moves too stiffly to avoid being stepped on by agile young April
29 female Q1; Q2 has *fennel* (an herb—supposed to be an aphrodisiac—strewn in the path of brides); either reading may be right, but the specificity of *fennel* as a particular kind of bud seems less congruous than *female* with the generalized spring image of 26-28
32-33 Which . . . none on a closer view of those attending (*lit.* "on more view of many of which," the vague antecedent of *which* being *all* (30), i.e. "all in attendance at the party"), you may conclude that my daughter, though she must be counted in the number, doesn't count in your esteem
34 sirrah familiar form of address, used mainly to children and servants
34 trudge "undignified equivalent of 'walk' " (OED), and thus well-suited to the presumed gracelessness of the Clown: see I iii 36
37 stay wait
39-41 that . . . nets i.e. that a man should stick to what he knows (but with the usual occupational attributes bumblingly reversed)
39 meddle . . . yard with a sexual quibble—see *meddle* (OED 3), *yard* (OED 10)
40 last wooden model used to shape shoes
44 In good time i.e. "in the nick of time" (spoken as he sees Benvolio and Romeo—gentry who will be able to read)
45 one . . . burning i.e. fire puts out fire (so let a new love affair put out the old)
46 another's another pain's
47 holp helped
48 with . . . languish i.e. as one succumbs to a new grief

Take thou some new infection to thy eye,
And the rank poison of the old will die. 50

ROMEO. Your plantain leaf is excellent for that.°

BENVOLIO. For what, I pray thee?

ROMEO. For your broken° shin.

BENVOLIO. Why, Romeo, art thou mad?

ROMEO. Not mad, but bound more than a madman is; 55
Shut up in prison, kept without my food,
Whipped and tormented° and—God-den,° good fellow.

SERVANT. God gi' go-den. I pray, sir, can you read?

ROMEO. Ay, mine own fortune in my misery.

SERVANT. Perhaps you have learned it without book.° But I 60
pray, can you read anything you see?

ROMEO. Ay, if I know the letters and the language.

SERVANT. Ye say honestly. Rest you merry.°

ROMEO. Stay, fellow; I can read. *He reads the letter.°*
'Signior Martino and his wife and daughters; 65
County Anselm and his beauteous sisters;
The lady widow of Vitruvio;
Signior Placentio and his lovely nieces;
Mercutio and his brother Valentine;
Mine uncle Capulet, his wife, and daughters; 70
My fair niece Rosaline and Livia;
Signior Valentio and his cousin Tybalt;
Lucio and the lively Helena.'
A fair assembly. Whither should they come?

SERVANT. Up. 75

ROMEO. Whither?

SERVANT. To supper; to our house.

ROMEO. Whose house?

SERVANT. My master's.

---

51 for that i.e. for healing minor skin-breaks (53) to which plantain was applied as a poultice (Romeo's implication is that the wounds of love are not healed so easily as Benvolio pretends)
53 broken skinned (see 51n)
55-57 bound . . . tormented measures held to be salutary for madness (see *Twelfth Night*, IV ii)
57 God-den good-e'en, i.e. good evening (a greeting used from noon on: see II iv 104)
60 without book by heart
63 Rest you merry construing Romeo to mean that he can read only if he has memorized in advance what is written, the servant starts to take leave
64 s.d. letter "anything written; inscription, document, text" (OED II i)

ROMEO. Indeed I should have asked thee that before. 80

SERVANT. Now I'll tell you without asking. My master is the great rich Capulet; and if you be not of the house of Montagues, I pray come and crush° a cup of wine. Rest you merry. [*Exit.*]

BENVOLIO. At this same ancient feast of Capulet's 85
Sups the fair Rosaline whom thou so loves;
With all the admirèd beauties of Verona.
Go thither, and with unattainted° eye
Compare her face with some that I shall show,
And I will make thee think thy swan a crow. 90

ROMEO. When the devout religion of mine eye
Maintains such falsehood, then turn tears to fires;
And these,° who, often drowned, could never die,
Transparent° heretics, be burnt for liars!°
One fairer than my love? The all-seeing sun 95
Ne'er saw her match since first the world begun.

BENVOLIO. Tut! you saw° her fair, none else being by,
Herself poised with herself in either eye;
But in that crystal scales let there be weighed
Your lady's love against some other maid° 100
That I will show you shining at this feast,
And she shall scant° show well that now seems best.

ROMEO. I'll go along, no such sight to be shown,
But to rejoice in splendor of my own.°
[*Exeunt.*]

---

83 crush humorous for "drink" (roughly = "annihilate")
88 unattainted uninfected (see 49-50), i.e., unprejudiced
91-94 When . . . liars when my eye (imaged here as a religious devotee) maintains such falsehood as to think any other object of worship equal or superior to Rosaline, then let my tears turn to fire and burn my eyes for heresy, just as religious heretics are burned for belying the truth
93 these i.e. these eyes (often drowned in tears)
94 Transparent (1) bright (as eyes) 2) obvious (as heretics)
97 saw i.e. judged
98-100 Herself . . . maid Romeo's eyes are compared to the two scales of a balance, first with an image of Rosaline in each, then with Rosaline and a rival
102 scant scarcely
104 my own i.e. Rosaline

Enter Capulet's Wife, and Nurse. I iii

LADY CAPULET. Nurse, where's my daughter? Call her forth to me.

NURSE. Now, by my maidenhead at twelve year old.°
I bade her come. What, lamb! what, ladybird!
God forbid,° where's this girl? What, Juliet!

Enter Juliet.

JULIET. How now? Who calls? 5

NURSE. Your mother.

JULIET. Madam, I am here. What is your will?

LADY CAPULET. This is the matter—Nurse, give leave° awhile,
We must talk in secret. Nurse, come back again;
I have rememb'red me, thou 's° hear our counsel. 10
Thou knowest my daughter's of a pretty age.

NURSE. Faith, I can tell her age unto an hour.

LADY CAPULET. She's not fourteen.

NURSE. I'll lay fourteen of my teeth—and yet, to my teen°
be it spoken, I have but four—she's not fourteen. 15
How long is it now to Lammastide?°

LADY CAPULET. A fortnight and odd days.

NURSE. Even or odd, of all days in the year,
Come Lammas Eve at night shall she be fourteen.
Susan° and she (God rest all Christian souls!) 20
Were of an age. Well, Susan is with God;
She was too good for me. But, as I said,
On Lammas Eve at night shall she be fourteen;
That shall she, marry;° I remember it well.

I iii 2ff Nurse..among the Nurse's speeches in this scene, lines 2-4, 14-16, 18-50, 52-59, 61-64, 69-70, 77-78 are printed as prose in Qq Ff, yet all but 14-16 are reasonably well-indicated on metrical grounds to have been composed as verse and are so printed by a majority of editors; lines 12, 80, 97, and 108 may be considered either prose or verse as printed in Qq Ff (since they occupy but one line each), but again on metrical grounds they may be confidently identified as verse; lines 14-16 remain a difficulty; since they do not assimilate to verse without a good deal of forcing, we have left them prose, as they are in Qq Ff, on the ground that there is variation between verse and prose in the Nurse's speeches throughout the play

2 at . . . old evidently the age at which she last had it
4 God forbid (1) the Nurse expresses annoyance with Juliet's failure to appear and mild apprehension lest something has happened to her? (2) the Nurse realizes that a possible meaning of ladybird (in addition to "sweetheart") is "light woman" and so hastens to disclaim it?
8 give leave leave us
10 thou 's thou shalt
14 teen sorrow
16 Lammastide August 1
20 Susan i.e. the Nurse's child (whose birth enabled her to nurse Juliet)
24 marry a mild oath: see I i 35n)

'Tis since the earthquake now eleven years; 25
And she was weaned (I never shall forget it),
Of all the days of the year, upon that day;
For I had then laid wormwood° to my dug,°
Sitting in the sun under the dovehouse wall.
My lord and you were then at Mantua. 30
Nay, I do bear a brain.° But, as I said,
When it did taste the wormwood on the nipple
Of my dug and felt it bitter, pretty fool,
To see it tetchy° and fall out° with the dug!
Shake, quoth the dovehouse!° 'Twas no need, I trow,° 35
To bid me trudge.°
And since that time it is eleven years,
For then she could stand high-lone;° nay, by th' rood,°
She could have run and waddled all about;
For even the day before, she broke° her brow; 40
And then my husband (God be with his soul!
'A° was a merry man) took up the child.
'Yea,' quoth he, 'dost thou fall upon thy face?
Thou wilt fall backward when thou hast more wit;°
Wilt thou not, Jule?' and, by my holidam,° 45
The pretty wretch left crying and said 'Ay.'
To see now how a jest shall come about!°
I warrant, an I should live a thousand years,
I never should forget it. 'Wilt thou not, Jule?' quoth he,
And, pretty fool, it stinted° and said 'Ay.' 50

LADY CAPULET. Enough of this. I pray thee hold thy peace.

NURSE. Yes, madam. Yet I cannot choose but laugh
To think it should leave crying and say 'Ay.'
And yet, I warrant, it had upon it° brow
A bump as big as a young cock'rel's stone;° 55

---

28 wormwood a bitter herb (applied to the Nurse's nipple to make Juliet give up nursing)
28 dug nipple
31 bear a brain have a keen mind
34 tetchy peevish
34 fall out quarrel
35 Shake . . . dovehouse the Nurse humorously dramatizes the scene and makes the dovehouse an actor in it
35 I trow *lit.* I trust (i.e. "I can tell you!")
36 trudge run: see I ii 34n
38 high-lone all alone
38 rood cross
40 broke skinned
42 'A he
44 wit sense
45 by my holidam a mild oath, originally by some holy relic or other sacred object
47 about i.e. true (since now Juliet is to be married)
50 stinted stopped crying
54 it its
55 stone testicle

A perilous knock; and it cried bitterly.
'Yea,' quoth my husband, 'fall'st upon thy face?
Thou wilt fall backward when thou comest to age;
Wilt thou not, Jule?' It stinted and said 'Ay.'

JULIET. And stint thou too, I pray thee, nurse, say I.° 60

NURSE. Peace, I have done. God mark° thee to his grace!
Thou wast the prettiest babe that e'er I nursed.
An I might live to see thee married once,
I have my wish.

LADY CAPULET. Marry, that 'marry' is the very theme 65
I came to talk of. Tell me, daughter Juliet,
How stands your dispositions to be married?

JULIET. It is an honor that I dream not of.

NURSE. An honor? Were not I thine only nurse,
I would say thou hadst sucked wisdom from thy teat. 70

LADY CAPULET. Well, think of marriage now. Younger than you,
Here in Verona, ladies of esteem,
Are made already mothers. By my count,
I was your mother much upon these years°
That you are now a maid. Thus then in brief: 75
The valiant Paris seeks you for his love.

NURSE. A man, young lady! lady, such a man
As all the world—why he's a man of wax.°

LADY CAPULET. Verona's summer hath not such a flower.°

NURSE. Nay, he's a flower, in faith—a very flower. 80

LADY CAPULET. What say you? Can you love the gentleman?
This night you shall behold him at our feast.
Read o'er the volume° of young Paris' face,
And find delight writ there with beauty's pen;
Examine every married lineament,° 85

---

60 say I with, of course, a quibble on the *Ay* in 46, 50, 53, 59
61 mark designate
74 much . . . years at about the same age (this makes Juliet's mother roughly 28 in Shakespeare's mind at this point; yet in some Q2 speech headings in this very scene she is "Old Lady," and later she herself speaks of her "old age": V iii 212 and note)
78 man of wax i.e. perfection—as if a model in wax (but perhaps with the ironic implication on Shakespeare's part that he is only a lifeless conventional "figure")
79 such a flower i.e. another flower equal to him
83 volume a metaphor that Lady Capulet expands in 84-94
85 married lineament well-matched feature

And see how one another lends content;°
And what obscured in this fair volume lies
Find written in the margent of his eyes.°
This precious book of love, this unbound° lover,
To beautify him only lacks a cover.° 90
The fish lives in the sea, and 'tis much pride
For fair–without the fair–within to hide.°
That book° in many's eyes doth share the glory,
That in gold clasps locks in the golden story;
So shall you share all that he doth possess, 95
By having him making yourself no less.

NURSE. No less? Nay, bigger!° Women grow by men.

LADY CAPULET. Speak briefly, can you like of° Paris' love?

JULIET. I'll look to like,° if looking liking move;
But no more deep will I endart° mine eye 100
Than your consent gives strength to make it fly.

Enter Servingman.

SERVINGMAN. Madam, the guests are come, supper served up, you called, my young lady asked for, the nurse cursed° in the pantry, and everything in extremity. I must hence to wait.° I beseech you follow straight.° 105

LADY CAPULET. We follow thee. [*Exit Servingman.*] Juliet, the County stays.°

NURSE. Go, girl, seek happy nights to happy days. *Exeunt.*

---

86 how . . . content how each enhances the other (with a pun on *content* = pleasure and *content* = contents of a book)
88 margent . . . eyes i.e. the commentary or gloss (so-called from the margin, where in older books it usually appeared) provided by his eyes
89 unbound (1) without a binding (considered as a book) (2) not yet captured (considered as a lover)
90 a cover i.e. a wife (to embrace him as a binding does a book)
91-92 The fish . . . hide a puzzling speech, usually interpreted to mean either (1) that as it is part of the universal order of things for a fish to live contained in the sea, its natural element, so it is equally part of the universal order for an attractive man to live contained by his natural element, an attractive woman; or (2) that the fish destined to serve for the "cover" of this "volume" (fish skin being often used to bind books) already exists, whether Juliet or another, and will share in the glory that results when a fine binding *(fair-without)* is conjoined with a fine content *(fair-within)*
93 book here used to mean the binding, or the book considered as a physical object (wtih *gold clasps* to hold its covers shut) as distinct from its story
97 bigger i.e. through pregnancy
98 like of favor
99 look to like look with favor
100 endart shoot my glance like a dart
103 cursed because she is not helping
105 wait serve
105 straight immediately
107 stays awaits you

Enter Romeo, Mercutio, Benvolio, with five or six other Maskers; Torchbearers. I iv

ROMEO. What, shall this speech be spoke for our excuse?°
Or shall we on without apology?

BENVOLIO. The date is out of such prolixity.°
We'll have no Cupid hoodwinked° with a scarf,
Bearing a Tartar's painted bow of lath,° 5
Scaring the ladies like a crowkeeper;°
[Nor no without-book° prologue, faintly spoke
After the prompter, for our entrance;°]
But, let them measure° us by what they will,
We'll measure them a measure° and be gone. 10

ROMEO. Give me a torch.° I am not for this ambling.°
Being but heavy,° I will bear the light.

MERCUTIO. Nay, gentle Romeo, we must have you dance.

ROMEO. Not I, believe me. You have dancing shoes
With nimble soles; I have a soul of lead 15
So stakes me to the ground I cannot move.

MERCUTIO. You are a lover. Borrow Cupid's wings
And soar with them above a common bound.

ROMEO. I am too sore enpiercèd with his shaft
To soar with his light feathers; and so bound 20
I cannot bound° a pitch° above dull woe.
Under love's heavy burden do I sink.

MERCUTIO. And, to sink in it,° should you° burden love—
Too great oppression for a tender thing.

I iv 1 excuse gate-crashing maskers often introduced themselves with a wittily rhymed speech of apology—a fashion Benvolio claims is now out of date
3 prolixity longwindedness
4 hoodwinked blindfolded
5 Tartar's . . . lath lip-shaped (like Cupid's bow) and fake
6 crowkeeper scarecrow
7-8 from Q1
7 without-book memorized
8 entrance here trisyllabic
9 measure judge of
10 measure . . . measure dance one dance
11 torch i.e. he will be a spectator holding a light: see 35
11 ambling dancing
12 heavy sad (with quibble on *heavy/light*)
19-21 I am . . . bound Romeo plays on Mercutio's *bound* = limit with *bound* = dancing leap, and on his *soar* with *sore*
21 pitch height (*lit.* the peak of a falcon's flight before it swoops on its prey)
23 in it i.e. in love (considered as copulation)
23 should you you would

ROMEO. Is love a tender thing? It is too rough, 25
Too rude, too boist'rous, and it pricks like thorn.

MERCUTIO. If love be rough with you, be rough with love.
Prick love for pricking, and you beat love down.
Give me a case° to put my visage in.
A visor for a visor!° What care I 30
What curious eye doth quote° deformities?
Here are the beetle brows° shall blush° for me.

BENVOLIO. Come, knock and enter; and no sooner in
But every man betake him to his legs.°

ROMEO. A torch for me! Let wantons light of heart 35
Tickle the senseless° rushes° with their heels;
For I am proverbed with a grandsire phrase,°
I'll be a candle-holder and look on;
The game was ne'er so fair, and I am done.

MERCUTIO. Tut! dun's the mouse,° the constable's own 40
word!°
If thou art Dun°, we'll draw thee from the mire,°
Or (save–your–reverence°) love, wherein thou stickest
Up to the ears. Come, we burn daylight,° ho!

ROMEO. Nay, that's not so.°

---

29 case mask (but in this context, with an actor's pause after the word before defining the particular case intended, the word may also have kept its sexual sense = female sex organ)
30 A visor . . . visor Mercutio speaks of his face as already having the ugliness of a mask
31 quote note
32 beetle brows beetling (i.e. heavy and bristling) brows affixed to the mask
32 blush the mask is evidently red or pink
34 betake . . . legs take part in the dance
36 senseless without feeling—hence to *tickle* them (= "arouse desire") has no effect
36 rushes floor covering
37 grandsire phrase old saying (either the idea expressed in 38, "a good candle-holder proves a good gamester," i.e., not being in the game, he can't lose—or that expressed in 39, "when play is best it's time to leave")
40 dun's the mouse proverbial for "be still" (*lit.* be as invisible as a mouse is in the dark because its color is *dun*, i.e. dark greyish brown)
40 constable's own word i.e. the instruction given to his watchmen lying in wait for thieves
41 Dun stock name for any horse (whether dun or not)
41 mire horses often became mired on Elizabethan roads, but Mercutio may also allude to an indoor winter game in which each player struggled to lift a great log representing a horse stuck in mire
42 save . . . reverence (1) apology used in introducing a vulgar or offensive subject-matter (2) term for human feces. Mercutio's joshing of Romeo consists both in prefacing "love" with an apology ordinarily reserved for obscenities (sense 1 above) and in qualifying it with a phrase that associates the sexual act grossly and grotesquely with *mire* (sense 2): see *stickest . . . ears.* (The Q1 reading—*mire/Of this sir-reverence*—tends to blur sense)
43 burn daylight burn torches by day, i.e. waste time
44 not so Romeo, taking the literal sense, points out that they *don't* burn their torches by day

MERCUTIO. I mean, sir, in delay 45
We waste our lights° in vain, light lights° by day.
Take our good meaning,° for our judgment sits°
Five times in that ere once in our fine wits.°

ROMEO. And we mean well in going to this masque,
But 'tis no wit° to go. 50

MERCUTIO. Why, may one ask?

ROMEO. I dreamt a dream to-night.°

MERCUTIO. And so did I.

ROMEO. Well, what was yours?

MERCUTIO. That dreamers often lie.° 55

ROMEO. In bed asleep, while they do dream things true.

MERCUTIO.° O, then I see Queen Mab° hath been with you.
She is the fairies' midwife°, and she comes
In shape no bigger than an agate stone°
On the forefinger of an alderman, 60
Drawn with a team of little atomi°
Over men's noses as they lie asleep;
Her wagon spokes made of long spinners'° legs,

---

46 our lights (1) our talents (2) our torches

46 light lights Mercutio explains (with mock laborious patience, as if to a child?) what he earlier meant by saying *we burn daylight* (Q2 has *lights lights*; though the "s" of the first *lights* is an obvious compositor's duplication, most editors unnecessarily follow Q1's *like lampes,* which spoils the characteristic Mercutian and Shakespearean jingle of *lights . . . light lights)*

47-48 Take . . . wits a difficult passage, which may perhaps best be paraphrased as follows: "take our common-sense meaning, for our judgment is to be found five times in that for every once it may be found in (the verbal high jinks of) our more refined intellectual powers"

47 our . . . meaning i.e. what I mean rather than what I say

47 sits (1) like a judge? (2) like a wind sitting (i.e. blowing from) a particular quarter?

48 fine wits Qq and Ff; Malone's *five wits,* tempting for its characteristic Mercutian "point" and jingle (*Five times . . . five wits),* is adopted by most editors, and may be right; yet it is not easy to see why the *five wits,* whether interpreted to mean the five senses or the five so-called faculties of the mind (common sense, imagination, fantasy, judgment, memory), should be regarded as in some way antithetical to that *good meaning* with which *judgment* concurs; whereas it is very easy to see how the ingenuities of speech that result from *fine wits* (illustrated everywhere in this scene) might be so regarded

50 'tis no wit it makes no sense

52 to-night last night

55 lie fib (with a pun on lying abed)

57ff Mercutio though it serves many purposes, Mercutio's long speech is required in part by the need to create an illusion of elapsing time for the Capulet supper that runs from I iii 101 I vi

57 Mab probably to be identified with a great Queen in Irish legend named Mebd, but not without such qualification (appropriately in this context) as comes from *mab* = loose woman and *Queen* = queen = whore

58 fairies' midwife i.e. the one among the fairies who officiates during our sleep at the birth of dreams

59 agate stone the figure incised on the agate in a seal ring (such as a town official like an alderman would need for sealing messages or documents)

61 atomi tiny creatures (plural of Latin *atomus)*

63 spinners' spiders'

The cover, of the wings of grasshoppers;
Her traces,° of the smallest spider's web; 65
Her collars, of the moonshine's wat'ry beams;
Her whip, of cricket's bone; the lash, of film;°
Her wagoner, a small grey-coated° gnat,
Not half so big as a round little worm
Pricked from the lazy finger of a maid;° 70
Her chariot is an empty hazelnut,
Made by the joiner° squirrel or old grub,°
Time out o' mind the fairies' coachmakers.
And in this state° she gallops night by night
Through lovers' brains, and then they dream of love; 75
O'er courtiers' knees, that dream on curtsies straight;
O'er lawyers' fingers, who straight° dream on fees;
O'er ladies' lips, who straight on kisses dream,
Which oft the angry Mab with blisters plagues,
Because their breaths with sweetmeats tainted are. 80
Sometime she gallops o'er a courtier's nose,
And then dreams he of smelling out a suit;°
And sometime comes she with a tithe-pig's° tail
Tickling a parson's nose as 'a lies asleep,
Then dreams he of another benefice.° 85
Sometimes she driveth o'er a soldier's neck,
And then dreams he of cutting foreign throats,
Of breaches,° ambuscadoes,° Spanish blades,°
Of healths five fathom deep;° and then anon
Drums in his ear, at which he starts and wakes, 90
And being thus frighted, swears a prayer or two
And sleeps again. This is that very Mab

---

65 traces straps attaching the *collar* (see 66) worn by the animal to the vehicle
67 film filament (as from a web)
68 grey-coated i.e. wearing grey livery
69-70 worm . . . maid lazy girls were told that worms bred in idle fingers
72 joiner cabinet maker—humorously so called because in opening nutshells he creates "coaches" (real coaches had fine cabinet—i.e. "joining"—work)
72 grub the insect larva that also eats through nutshells
74 state i.e. splendor or style
77 straight immediately
82 suit i.e. a petitioner seeking royal approval for an enterprise and therefore willing to pay the courtier for his influence (as businesses today pay lobbyists)
83 tithe-pig to be claimed as part of the tithe (i.e. the tenth part of agricultural produce due from each parishioner for support of the church)
85 another benefice additional church position
88 breaches i.e. in the city walls being assaulted
88 ambuscadoes ambushes
88 Spanish blades swords from Spain (in Shakespeare's time, home of the finest steels)
89 healths . . . deep toasts drunk from vast tankards (*lit.* 30 feet deep)

That plats° the manes of horses in the night
And bakes° the elflocks° in foul sluttish hairs,
Which once untangled much misfortune bodes. 95
This is the hag°, when maids lie on their backs,
That presses them and learns them first to bear,°
Making them women of good carriage.°
This is she—

ROMEO. Peace, peace, Mercutio, peace! 100
Thou talk'st of nothing.

MERCUTIO. True, I talk of dreams;
Which are the children of an idle brain,
Begot of nothing but vain fantasy;°
Which is as thin of substance as the air, 105
And more inconstant than the wind, who woos
Even now the frozen bosom of the North
And, being angered,° puffs away from thence,
Turning his side to the dew-dropping° South.

BENVOLIO. This wind you talk of blows us from ourselves. 110
Supper is done, and we shall come too late.

ROMEO. I fear, too early; for my mind misgives
Some consequence,° yet hanging in the stars,°
Shall bitterly begin his fearful date
With this night's revels and expire the term 115
Of° a despisèd° life, closed in my breast,
By some vile forfeit of untimely death.
But he° that hath the steerage of my course
Direct my sail! On, lusty gentlemen!

BENVOLIO. Strike, drum. 120

---

93 plats tangles (*lit.* plaits, braids)
94 bakes i.e. cakes, solidifies
94 elflocks tangles supposedly made by elves (outraged by any form of slovenliness) in unkempt hair
96 hag witch (the nightmare demon)
97 bear i.e. (1) children (2) the weight of a man
98 carriage posture (but with a glance at carrying children and supporting the weight of a man)
104 vain fantasy empty fancy
108 angered i.e. by her "coldness" to him
109 dew-dropping rainy, fertile
113 consequence chain of events
113 yet . . . stars (see the emphasis on ill-fatedness in the Prologue sonnet)
115-16 expire . . . Of foreclose (as of a mortgage bond on which the specified *forfeit* (117) for non-payment is death)
116 despisèd because of his melancholy, hopeless love for Rosaline
118 he i.e. God

They march about the stage, and Servingmen come forth with napkins.° I v

1. SERVINGMAN. Where's Potpan, that he helps not to take away? He shift a trencher!° he scrape a trencher!

2. SERVINGMAN. When good manners° shall lie all in one or two men's hands, and they unwashed too, 'tis a foul thing.

1. SERVINGMAN. Away with the joint-stools,° remove the court-cupboard,° look to the plate. Good thou, save me a piece of marchpane° and, as thou loves me, let the porter let in Susan Grindstone and Nell.° [*Exit second Servingman.*] Anthony, and Potpan! 5

[*Enter two more Servingmen.*]

3. SERVINGMAN. Ay, boy, ready. 10

1. SERVINGMAN. You are looked for and called for, asked for and sought for, in the great chamber.

4. SERVINGMAN. We cannot be here and there too. Cheerly, boys! Be brisk awhile, and the longer liver take all.°

[*Exit third and fourth Servingmen.*]

Enter [*Capulet, his Wife, Juliet, Tybalt, Nurse, and*] *all the Guests and Gentlewomen to the Maskers.*

CAPULET. Welcome, gentlemen! Ladies that have their toes 15
Unplagued with corns will walk a bout° with you.
Ah ha, my mistresses! which of you all
Will now deny to dance? She that makes dainty,°
She I'll swear hath corns. Am I come near ye now?°
Welcome, gentlemen! I have seen the day 20
That I have worn a visor and could tell
A whispering tale in a fair lady's ear,

I v s.d. in Elizabethan stage practice "marching about" signifies a change of place—in this instance bringing the Maskers to a retired position at the back as the servants *come forth with napkins* for their brief interchange, at the end of which the Maskers again take stage center as the Capulet guests enter to greet them; there is no indication in Qq or Ff that the Maskers go offstage
2 trencher wooden plate
3 good manners i.e. common household decencies
5 joint-stools those made by a cabinet-maker and so to be kept for "best"
6 court-cupboard movable cabinet for displaying *plate* (= silverware)
7 marchpane marzipan, a candy made with almonds
8 Susan . . . Nell evidently invited to a servants' party in the kitchen
14 the . . . all proverbial incitement to enjoy oneself
16 walk a bout dance a turn
18 makes dainty pretends to shrink from it
19 Am . . . now have I sized you up

Such as would please. 'Tis gone, 'tis gone, 'tis gone!
You are welcome, gentlemen! Come, musicians, play.
Music plays, and they dance.

A hall,° a hall! give room! and foot it, girls. 25
More light, you knaves!° and turn the tables up,°
And quench the fire, the room is grown too hot.
Ah, sirrah, this unlooked-for sport°comes well.
Nay, sit, nay, sit, good cousin Capulet,
For you and I are past our dancing days. 30
How long is't now since last yourself and I
Were in a mask?

2. CAPULET. By'r Lady, thirty years.

CAPULET. What, man? 'Tis not so much, 'tis not so much;
'Tis since the nuptial of Lucentio, 35
Come Pentecost° as quickly as it will,
Some five-and-twenty years, and then we masked.

2. CAPULET. 'Tis more, 'tis more. His son is elder, sir;
His son is thirty.

CAPULET. Will you tell me that? 40
His son was but a ward° two years ago.

ROMEO. [*to a Servingman*] What lady's that, which doth enrich the hand
Of yonder knight?

SERVINGMAN. I know not, sir.

ROMEO. O, she doth teach the torches to burn bright! 45
It seems she hangs upon the cheek of night
As a rich jewel in an Ethiop's ear—
Beauty too rich for use, for earth too dear!°
So shows a snowy dove trooping with crows
As yonder lady o'er her fellows shows.° 50
The measure° done, I'll watch her place of stand

---

25 A hall i.e. clear the floor
26 knaves servants
26 turn . . . up dismount the boards from their trestles (so as to make space)
28 sport the Maskers' coming
36 Pentecost Whitsunday (the seventh after Easter)
41 ward minor
48 Beauty . . . dear a speech richer in implications and premonitions than its speaker can yet be aware (*Beauty* probably contains a pun on "booty," which was pronounced very much the same; *too rich for use* may mean both "beyond price" and "too fine or delicate for the wear and tear of a humdrum existence"; *earth* may mean both "mortal life" and "the grave"—where Juliet's beauty is all too speedily to be found; and *dear* may mean, as we have found earlier, "costly" as well as "prized")
49-50 So . . . shows see I ii 90
51 measure dance figure

And, touching hers, make blessèd my rude° hand.
Did my heart love till now? Forswear it, sight!
For I ne'er saw true beauty till this night.

TYBALT. This, by his voice, should be a Montague. 55
Fetch me my rapier, boy. [*His Page goes out.*] What,
dares the slave
Come hither, covered with an antic face,°
To fleer° and scorn at our solemnity?°
Now, by the stock and honor of my kin,°
To strike him dead I hold it not a sin. 60

CAPULET. Why, how now, kinsman? Wherefore storm you
so?

TYBALT. Uncle, this is a Montague, our foe;
A villain, that is hither come in spite
To scorn at our solemnity this night.

CAPULET. Young Romeo is it? 65

TYBALT. 'Tis he, that villain Romeo.

CAPULET. Content thee, gentle coz, let him alone.
'A bears him like a portly° gentleman,
And, to say truth, Verona brags of him
To be a virtuous and well-governed youth. 70
I would not for the wealth of all this town
Here in my house do him disparagement.
Therefore be patient, take no note of him.
It is my will, the which if thou respect,
Show a fair presence° and put off these frowns. 75
An ill-beseeming semblance for a feast.

TYBALT. It fits° when such a villain is a guest.
I'll not endure him.

CAPULET. He shall be endured.
What, goodman° boy! I say he shall. Go to!° 80
Am I the master here, or you? Go to!

---

52 rude rough (in comparison with hers)
57 antic face grotesque mask
58 fleer smile contemptuously
58 solemnity feast
59 the stock . . . kin the honor of the stock I spring from
68 portly of good deportment
75 fair presence friendly, well-behaved bearing
77 fits Tybalt responds to Capulet's *ill-beseeming = unfitting*
80 goodman term applied to one below the rank of gentleman (suited here to Tybalt, Capulet implies, because he lacks a gentleman's self-restraint: see also *boy*)
80 Go to common expression of impatience

You'll not endure him, God shall mend my soul!°
You'll make a mutiny° among my guests!
You will set cock-a-hoop,° you'll be the man!°

TYBALT. Why, uncle, 'tis a shame. 85

CAPULET.° Go to, go to!
You are a saucy° boy. Is't so, indeed?
This trick° may chance to scathe° you. I know what.°
You must contrary me! Marry, 'tis time°—
Well said, my hearts!°—You are a princox:° go, 90
Be quiet, or—More light, more light!—For shame!
I'll make you quiet; what!—Cheerly, my hearts!

TYBALT. [*aside*] Patience perforce with willful choler meeting
Makes my flesh tremble in their different greeting.°
I will withdraw; but this intrusion shall, 95
Now seeming sweet,° convert to bitt'rest gall. *Exit.*

ROMEO. [*Takes Juliet's hand.*] If I profane with my unworthiest hand
This holy shrine,° the gentle sin° is this;
My lips, two blushing pilgrims,° ready stand
To smooth that rough touch with a tender kiss. 100

JULIET. Good pilgrim, you do wrong your hand too much,
Which mannerly devotion shows in this;
For saints have hands that pilgrims' hands do touch,
And palm to palm is holy palmer's° kiss.°

---

82 God . . . soul equally an expression of impatience
83 mutiny riot
84 set cock-a-hoop let mischief loose (from setting open the spigot *(cock)* of the barrel *(hoop)* so as to let the contents flow freely: see *set abroach,* I i 100 and note)
84 be the man i.e. "act like Mr. Big"
86 Capulet here he addresses Tybalt and the dancers alternately, seeking to keep his altercation with the former from the notice of the latter; just possibly his *Is't so indeed?* is addressed to a guest or to "2. Capulet" rather than to Tybalt
87 saucy insolent
88 trick Capulet evidently gives Tybalt a box on the ear, a usual punishment for unruly boys and hence doubly insulting
88 scathe hurt
88 what what I'm doing (i.e. in insisting Romeo's presence be ignored)
89 time (1) time to put you in your place? (2) time you were forced out of here? (3) a fine time to contrary me (spoken with sarcasm)?
90 Well . . . hearts "well-done, dancers" (i.e. don't be disturbed at what is going on between Tybalt and me)
90 princox impudent fellow
93-94 Patience . . . greeting my enforced endurance (of this invasion of our house by a Montague) collides with the anger I feel at it to make my flesh tremble
96 seeming sweet i.e. to the invading Romeo
98 shrine i.e. Juliet's hand (which Romeo has taken)
98 the . . . sin i.e. as opposed to what Romeo affects to consider the *less* gentle sin of profaning her soft hand by taking it in his rougher one, the *gentle* sin will be to kiss it (his lips being presumably as soft as it is) and so repair the wrong
99 pilgrims i.e. because, like pilgrims, his lips seek a shrine
104 palmers pilgrims carrying palm fronds to show they had been to the Holy Land
101-4 Good . . . kiss i.e. you have done no wrong (by taking my hand) but shown only permissible devotion; for the hands of pilgrims do appropriately clasp the hands of effigies of saints, and the kiss of palmers is rightly palm to palm

ROMEO. Have not saints lips, and holy palmers too? 105

JULIET. Ay, pilgrim, lips that they must use in prayer.°

ROMEO. O, then, dear saint, let lips do what hands do!°
They pray; grant thou, lest faith turn to despair.°

JULIET. Saints do not move,° though grant for prayers' sake.

ROMEO. Then move not° while my prayer's effect° I take. 110
Thus from my lips, by thine my sin is purged. [*Kisses her.*]

JULIET. Then have my lips the sin that they have took.

ROMEO. Sin from my lips? O trespass sweetly urged!
Give me my sin again. [*Kisses her.*]

JULIET. You kiss by th' book.° 115

NURSE. Madam, your mother craves a word with you.

ROMEO. What is her mother?

NURSE. Marry, bachelor,
Her mother is the lady of the house,
And a good lady, and a wise and virtuous. 120
I nursed her daughter that you talked withal.°
I tell you, he that can lay hold of her
Shall have the chinks.°

ROMEO. Is she a Capulet?
O dear° account!° my life is my foe's debt.° 125

BENVOLIO. Away, be gone; the sport is at the best.°

ROMEO. Ay, so I fear; the more is my unrest.

CAPULET. Nay, gentlemen, prepare not to be gone;
We have a trifling foolish banquet° towards.°
[*They whisper in his ear.*°]
Is it e'en so? Why then, I thank you all. 130
I thank you, honest gentlemen. Good night.
More torches here! Come on then, let's to bed.

---

106 in prayer i.e. rather than in kissing
107 what . . . do i.e. touch
108 despair with allusion also (in this context) to the despair of salvation that afflicts the religiously devout
109 move take the initiative
110 move not stand still
110 effect fulfillment
115 by th' book authoritatively (1) as if you had mastered the art from some acknowledged guide (2) as if (in your pilgrim approach) you had the whole weight of the "book" (Bible) on your side
121 withal with
123 chinks coins (i.e. riches)
125 dear costly, grievous
125 account statement of assets and obligations
125 my foe's debt i.e. owed to Juliet, who is my foe
126 Away . . . best see I iv 39 and I iv 37n
129 banquet light supper
129 towards in preparation
129 s.d. They . . . ear from Q1

Ah, sirrah, by my fay,° it waxes late;
I'll to my rest. [*Exeunt all but Juliet and Nurse.*]

JULIET. Come hither, nurse. What is yond gentleman? 135

NURSE. The son and heir of old Tiberio.

JULIET. What's he that now is going out of door?

NURSE. Marry, that, I think, be young Petruchio.°

JULIET. What's he that follows there, that would not dance?

NURSE. I know not. 140

JULIET. Go ask his name.—If he be marriè̀d,
My grave is like to be my wedding bed.

NURSE. His name is Romeo, and a Montague,
The only son of your great enemy.

JULIET. My only love, sprung from my only hate! 145
Too early seen unknown, and known too late!
Prodigious° birth of love it is to me
That I must love a loathèd enemy.

NURSE. What's this? what's this?

JULIET. A rhyme I learnt even now 150
Of one I danced withal. *One calls within,* 'Juliet.'

NURSE. Anon,° anon!
Come, let's away; the strangers all are gone. *Exeunt.*

II Prologue°

[*Enter*] *Chorus.*

[CHORUS]. Now old desire° doth in his deathbed lie,
And young affection gapes° to be his heir;

---

133 fay faith
138 Petruchio the *ch* is pronounced as in *much*
147 Prodigious monstrous
152 Anon at once
II Prologue the justification for this second prologue "is not easily discovered" (to use Samuel Johnson's words) since the lines tell us nothing we do not already know or cannot easily anticipate. Though it has been suggested that they were written to cover the removal of stools and other furniture needed for I v, this seems less likely (since the four servants at I v 1ff could have performed this function) than that a need was again felt to give a sense of elapsing time between Romeo's departure from the ball at the end of I v and his reappearance at II i 1-2
1 old desire i.e. for Rosaline
2 gapes longs (*lit.* opens his jaws hungrily)

That fair for which love groaned for and would die,
With tender Juliet matched, is now not fair.
Now Romeo is beloved and loves again,
Alike° bewitchèd by the charm of looks; 5
But to his foe supposed he must complain,°
And she steal love's sweet bait from fearful° hooks.
Being held a foe, he may not have access
To breathe such vows as lovers use° to swear, 10
And she as much in love, her means much less
To meet her new belovèd anywhere;
But passion lends them power, time means, to meet,
Temp'ring extremities° with extreme sweet. [*Exit.*]

Enter Romeo alone. **IIi**

ROMEO. Can I go forward when my heart is here?°
Turn back, dull earth,° and find thy center° out.
Enter Benvolio with Mercutio. [*Romeo retires.*]

BENVOLIO. Romeo! my cousin Romeo! Romeo!

MERCUTIO. He is wise, and, on my life, hath stol'n him home to bed. 5

BENVOLIO. He ran this way and leapt this orchard° wall.
Call, good Mercutio.

MERCUTIO. Nay, I'll conjure° too.
Romeo! humors!° madman! passion! lover!
Appear thou in the likeness of a sigh; 10
Speak but one rhyme, and I am satisfied!
Cry but 'Ay me!' pronounce but 'love' and 'dove';
Speak to my gossip Venus° one fair word,

---

6 **Alike** i.e. both lovers alike
7 **complain** address his appeals
8 **fearful** frightening
10 **use** are accustomed
14 **Temp'ring extremities** i.e. mixing hardships

II i 1 my . . . here i.e. the Petrarchan lover's insistence that his heart remains with the beloved
2 **earth** i.e. his body
2 **center** his heart, which is with Juliet ((but alluding to the supposed tendency of all things having weight to come to rest in "the center," i.e. earth's center regarded as the center of the entire universe
6 **orchard** garden (but obviously one containing fruit-trees: see 36-38)
8 **conjure** i.e. like a magician (calling up a spirit who will appear only if the magician hits on the right name—hence the several names in 9)
9 **humors** whims (i.e. "Mr. Changeable")
10-16 Appear . . . maid mockery of the conventional melancholy lover's behavior, such as Romeo shows in I i
13 **my . . . Venus** i.e. "Your pal, Venus" —with whom Romeo is imagined by Mercutio to be on an easy footing (gossip—derived from god = God + sib = related—originally meant godfather or godmother, then any person with whom one was on familiar chit-chatting terms)

One nickname for her purblind° son and heir
Young Abraham Cupid,° he that shot so true 15
When King Cophetua loved the beggar maid!°
He heareth not, he stirreth not, he moveth not;
The ape is dead,° and I must conjure him.
I conjure thee by Rosaline's bright eyes,
By her high forehead and her scarlet lip, 20
By her fine foot, straight leg, and quivering thigh,
And the demesnes° that there adjacent lie,
That in thy likeness thou appear to us!

BENVOLIO. An if he hear thee, thou wilt anger him.

MERCUTIO. This cannot anger him. 'Twould anger him 25
To raise a spirit in his mistress' circle°
Of some strange° nature, letting it there stand
Till she had laid it and conjured it down.
That were some spite; my invocation
Is fair and honest: in his mistress' name, 30
I conjure only but to raise up him.

BENVOLIO. Come, he hath hid himself among these trees
To be consorted with° the humorous° night.
Blind is his love and best befits the dark.

MERCUTIO. If love be blind, love cannot hit the mark.° 35
Now will he sit under a medlar tree
And wish his mistress were that kind of fruit
As maids call medlars° when they laugh alone.°
O, Romeo, that she were, O that she were

---

14 purblind (1) blind (2) stupid
15 Abraham Cupid so called (as being a deceiver, trickster, and scapegrace) from "Abraham Man," a name given to a class of beggars and thieves who wandered about half-naked (like Cupid); Mercutio may also intend a witty antithesis between *young* and *Abraham*, the venerable Old Testament patriarch
16 When . . . maid alluding to the subject of a popular ballad, in which King Cophetua makes a beggar-maid his queen
18 ape is dead i.e. like a performing ape trained to play dead until aroused by a certain formula (Mercutio's "formula" follows in 19-22)
22 demesnes regions
26 circle i.e. the "magic circle" within which a spirit is raised by a conjurer—but of course with a ribald innuendo that carries over to *stand* (27), *laid . . . down* (28), *raise up* (31)
27 strange alien (i.e. belonging to someone other than Romeo)
33 consorted with companioned by
33 humorous (1) damp (when taken to describe *night* as the period between sunset and sunrise) (2) moody (when taken to describe *night* personified as Romeo's companion, as full of *humors* as he: see 9n)
35 hit the mark with the usual sexual implication: see I i 209
38 medlars small brown apples (from their shape called open-arses)
38 alone in privacy together

An open—or° thou a pop'rin pear!° 40
Romeo, good night. I'll to my truckle-bed;°
This field-bed is too cold for me to sleep.
Come, shall we go?

BENVOLIO. Go then, for 'tis in vain
To seek him here that means not to be found. 45

Exit [*with Mercutio*].

II ii

ROMEO. [*coming forward*] He jests at scars that never felt a wound.

[*Enter Juliet above at a window.*]

But soft! What light through yonder window breaks?
It is the East, and Juliet is the sun!
Arise, fair sun, and kill the envious moon,
Who is already sick and pale with grief 5
That thou her maid° art far more fair than she.
Be not her maid,° since she is envious.
Her vestal° livery is but sick and green,°
And none but fools do wear it. Cast it off.
It is my lady, O it is my love, O that she knew she were!° 10
She speaks, yet she says nothing. What of that?

---

40 open—or Q1 has *open et cetera* (*et cetera* being a stock euphemism for the female sex organ), which many editors adopt despite its effect on the rhythm of the line. Q2 has *open or*, which some emend to *open-arse* or to *open-arse and;* we follow Q2 (inserting only a dash to represent an actor's knowing pause), on the ground that, after the clear evocation of the vulgarism for medlar in 38, it is wittier and more Mercutian in 40—and certainly more effective theatrically—to dangle it before the mind than to speak it outright; further, there seems no necessity to emend Q2 *or* to *and:* if Rosaline (says Mercutio) were *such fruit as maids call medlars when they laugh alone*, or, contrariwise, if you were *a pop'rin pear*, you would have your wish

40 pop'rin pear so-called from Poperinge, its place of origin in west Belgium, and associated with the male sex organ both from its name and its appearance.

41 truckle-bed a low bed on truckles (= castors) that can be shoved under a high bed when not in use

II ii 6 her maid i.e. her virgin votaress (since Diana, goddess of the moon, was patroness of virgins)

7 Be . . . maid put away your virgin state

8 vestal i.e. virginal (from the virgin devotees of Vesta, Roman goddess of the hearth)

8 sick and green alluding to the color sometimes seen in the moon ("the moon is made of green cheese"), but also to the green-sickness—"an anemic disease which mostly affects young women about the age of puberty and gives a pale and greenish tinge to the complexion" (OED)

10 It . . . were most edtiors print as one pentameter line plus a fragment (ending *love/were*), but the Qq Ff lineation, which we preserve together with its punctuation, perhaps better expresses Romeo's impetuous rapture

Her eye discourses; I will answer it.
I am too bold; 'tis not to me she speaks.
Two of the fairest stars in all the heaven,
Having some business, do entreat her eyes 15
To twinkle in their spheres° till they return.
What if her eyes were there, they in her head?
The brightness of her cheek would shame those stars
As daylight doth a lamp; her eyes in heaven
Would through the airy region stream so bright 20
That birds would sing and think it were not night.
See how she leans her cheek upon her hand!
O that I were a glove upon that hand,
That I might touch that cheek!

JULIET. Ay me! 25

ROMEO. She speaks.
O, speak again, bright angel! for thou art
As glorious to this night, being o'er my head,
As is a wingèd messenger of heaven
Unto the white-upturnèd° wond'ring eyes 30
Of mortals that fall back to gaze on him
When he bestrides the lazy puffing° clouds
And sails upon the bosom of the air.

JULIET. O Romeo, Romeo! wherefore° art thou Romeo?
Deny thy father and refuse thy name; 35
Or, if thou wilt not, be but sworn my love,
And I'll no longer be a Capulet.

ROMEO. [*aside*] Shall I hear more, or shall I speak at this?

---

10 O that . . . were the likeness of this in form and sound to II i 34-40 calls to mind the vast abyss that separates the two in content
16 spheres i.e. the concentric transparent spheres that, in Ptolemaic astronomy, the planets were presumed to be fixed in
30 white-upturnèd i.e. showing the white of the eye as it rolls upward to look
32 puffing the image seems to be drawn from the representation of winds in old maps as clouds with cheeks puffed out, perhaps with reference also to the hint of puffed-out canvas that lurks in *sails* in 33 (Q1 has *pacing*, which many editors accept because *bestrides* suggests a *steed*, or emend to *passing* in the belief that puffing is a compositor's misreading of *passing*; though these are reasonable conjectures, nothing requires them)
34 wherefore why

JULIET. 'Tis but thy name that is my enemy.
Thou art thyself, though not a Montague.° 40
What's Montague? It is nor hand, nor foot,
Nor arm, nor face, nor any other part
Belonging to a man. O, be some other name!°
What's in a name? That which we call a rose
By any other name would smell as sweet. 45
So Romeo would, were he not Romeo called,
Retain that dear perfection which he owes°
Without that title. Romeo, doff° thy name;
And for thy name, which is no part of thee,
Take all myself. 50

ROMEO. I take thee at thy word.
Call me but love, and I'll be new baptized;
Henceforth I never will be Romeo.

JULIET. What man art thou that, thus bescreened in night,
So stumblest on my counsel?° 55

ROMEO. By a name
I know not how to tell thee who I am.
My name, dear saint, is hateful to myself,
Because it is an enemy to thee.
Had I it written, I would tear the word. 60

JULIET. My ears have yet not drunk a hundred words
Of thy tongue's uttering, yet I know the sound.
Art thou not Romeo, and a Montague?

ROMEO. Neither, fair maid, if either thee dislike.°

JULIET. How camest thou hither, tell me, and wherefore? 65
The orchard walls are high and hard to climb,

---

40 Thou . . . Montague a confusing sentence, which may be interpreted in two ways, neither entirely satisfactory: (1) "You would be yourself even if you were not a Montague"—unsatisfactory in sense because the context seems to demand and Juliet to intend: "You are yourself even if you are a Montague"; (2) "You are yourself, though, not a Montague"—unsatisfactory in grammar because *though* in this sense implies something antithetical to what has gone before, not something that is a parallel or a simple expansion, as in this case; and perhaps unsatisfactory too in being a usage of *though* with few Shakespearean precedents (see, however, *A Midsummer Night's Dream,* III ii 356-57, "Your hands than mine are quicker for a fray,/My legs are longer, though, to run away); on balance, the second interpretation is perhaps to be preferred

42-43 Nor . . . name..Q2 has: *Nor arme, nor face, O be some other name/Belonging to a man./What's,* etc. Q1 has: *Nor arme, nor face, nor any other part./What's,* etc. The present text, a conflation first made by Malone, is now almost universally accepted despite the hexameter it makes of 43

47 owes owns

48 doff "do off," i.e. put off

55 counsel secret meditations

64 dislike displease

And the place death, considering who thou art,
If any of my kinsmen find thee here.

ROMEO. With love's light wings did I o'erperch° these walls;
For stony limits cannot hold love out, 70
And what love can do, that dares love attempt.
Therefore thy kinsmen are no stop to me.

JULIET. If they do see thee, they will murder thee.

ROMEO. Alack, there lies more peril in thine eye
Than twenty of their swords! Look thou but sweet, 75
And I am proof° against their enmity.

JULIET. I would not for the world they saw thee here.

ROMEO. I have night's cloak to hide me from their eyes;
And but thou love me, let them find me here.°
My life were better ended by their hate 80
Than death proroguèd,° wanting of thy love.

JULIET. By whose direction found'st thou out this place?

ROMEO. By love, that first did prompt me to inquire.
He lent me counsel, and I lent him eyes.
I am no pilot; yet, wert thou as far 85
As that vast shore washed with the farthest sea,
I should adventure° for such merchandise.

JULIET. Thou knowest the mask of night is on my face;
Else would a maiden blush bepaint my cheek
For that which thou hast heard me speak to-night. 90
Fain° would I dwell on form°—fain, fain deny
What I have spoke; but farewell compliment!°
Dost thou love me? I know thou wilt say 'Ay';°
And I will take thy word. Yet, if thou swear'st,
Thou mayst prove false. At lovers' perjuries, 95
They say Jove laughs. O gentle Romeo,
If thou dost love, pronounce it faithfully.
Or if thou thinkest I am too quickly won,

---

69 **o'erperch** fly over
76 **proof** armored
79 **but . . . here** i.e. unless you love me, why should I care to live
81 **proroguèd** postponed
87 **adventure** risk a voyage (like the merchant adventurers—contemporary speculators who pooled their assets to fit out ships for voyages of gain)
91 **Fain** gladly
91 **form** decorum
92 **compliment** conventional social behavior
93 **thou . . . 'Ay'** as in 10, above, Shakespeare possibly means to define the quality of the moment by reminding us of a different one: I iii 37-60

I'll frown, and be perverse, and say thee nay,
So° thou wilt woo; but else, not for the world. 100
In truth, fair Montague, I am too fond,°
And therefore thou mayst think my havior° light;
But trust me, gentleman, I'll prove more true
Than those that have more cunning to be strange.°
I should have been more strange, I must confess, 105
But that thou overheard'st, ere I was ware,°
My true-love passion. Therefore pardon me,
And not impute this yielding to light° love,
Which the dark night hath so discoverèd.°

ROMEO. Lady, by yonder blessèd moon I vow, 110
That tips with silver all these fruit-tree tops—

JULIET. O, swear not by the moon, th' inconstant moon,
That monthly changes in her circled orb,
Lest that thy love prove likewise variable.

ROMEO. What shall I swear by? 115

JULIET. Do not swear at all;
Or if thou wilt, swear by thy gracious self,
Which is the god of my idolatry,
And I'll believe thee.

ROMEO. If my heart's dear love— 120

JULIET. Well, do not swear. Although I joy in thee,
I have no joy of this contract° to-night.
It is too rash, too unadvised, too sudden;
Too like the lightning, which doth cease to be
Ere one can say 'It lightens.' Sweet, good night! 125
This bud of love, by summer's ripening breath,
May prove a beauteous flow'r when next we meet.
Good night, good night! As sweet repose and rest
Come to thy heart as that within my breast!

ROMEO. O, wilt thou leave me so unsatisfied? 130

JULIET. What satisfaction canst thou have to-night?

ROMEO. Th' exchange of thy love's vow for mine.

---

100 So i.e. provided that
101 fond foolishly affectionate
102 havior behavior
104 be strange i.e. play hard-to-get
106 ware aware of your presence
108 light i.e. shallow (but with an antithetical play on *dark* in 109)
109 discoverèd made known
122 contract Elizabethan term for betrothal, an exchange of vows that legally and morally had the status of marriage, apart from connubial rights

JULIET. I gave thee mine before thou didst request it;
And yet I would it were to give again.

ROMEO. Wouldst thou withdraw it? For what purpose, love? 135

JULIET. But to be frank° and give it thee again.
And yet I wish but for the thing I have.
My bounty° is as boundless as the sea,
My love as deep; the more I give to thee,
The more I have, for both are infinite. 140
I hear some noise within. Dear love, adieu!
[*Nurse calls within*°.]
Anon, good nurse! Sweet Montague, be true.
Stay but a little, I will come again. [*Exit.*]

ROMEO. O blessèd, blessèd night! I am afeard,
Being in night, all this is but a dream, 145
Too flattering-sweet to be substantial.

[*Enter Juliet above.*]

JULIET. Three words, dear Romeo, and good night indeed.
If that thy bent° of love be honorable,
Thy purpose marriage, send me word to-morrow,
By one that I'll procure to come to thee, 150
Where and what time thou wilt perform the rite;
And all my fortunes at thy foot I'll lay
And follow thee my lord throughout the world.

NURSE. [*within*] Madam!

JULIET. I come, anon.—But if thou meanest not well, 155
I do beseech thee—

NURSE. [*within*] Madam!

JULIET. By and by° I come.—
To cease thy suit and leave me to my grief.
To-morrow will I send. 160

ROMEO. So thrive my soul—

JULIET. A thousand times good night! [*Exit.*]

ROMEO. A thousand times the worse, to want thy light!°

---

136 frank (1) generous (with love) (2) forthright (in speech)
138 bounty desire and capacity to give
141 s.d. within i.e. from offstage
148 bent aim (from the bending of a bow)
158 By and by immediately
163 A . . . light i.e. night is a thousand times worse now that it lacks the light radiating from Juliet

Love goes toward love as schoolboys from their books;
But love from love, toward school with heavy looks. 165

Enter Juliet [*above*] *again.*

JULIET. Hist!° Romeo, hist! O for a falc'ner's voice
To lure this tassel-gentle° back again!
Bondage° is hoarse° and may not speak aloud,
Else would I tear the cave where Echo lies°
And make her airy tongue more hoarse than mine 170
With repetition of 'My Romeo!'

ROMEO. It is my soul that calls upon my name.
How silver-sweet sound lovers' tongues by night,
Like softest music to attending° ears!

JULIET. Romeo! 175

ROMEO. My dear?°

JULIET. What o'clock to-morrow
Shall I send to thee?

ROMEO. By the hour of nine.

JULIET. I will not fail. 'Tis twenty years till then. 180
I have forgot why I did call thee back.

ROMEO. Let me stand here till thou remember it.

JULIET. I shall forget, to have thee still stand there,
Rememb'ring how I love thy company.

ROMEO. And I'll still stay, to have thee still forget, 185
Forgetting any other home but this.

JULIET. 'Tis almost morning. I would have thee gone—
And yet no farther than a wanton's° bird,
That lets it hop a little from her hand,
Like a poor prisoner in his twisted gyves,° 190

---

166 Hist "a sibilant exclamation used to enjoin silence, attract attention, or call on people to listen"—OED (but used here with special reference to the calling of falcons)
167 tassel-gentle tercel gentle, or male falcon
168 Bondage i.e. Juliet's condition as a young unmarried daughter in an Elizabethan household (see e.g. II v 67)
168 hoarse i.e. unable to give voice
169 cave . . . lies for love of Narcissus, the nymph Echo pined away in her cave to a mere voice
174 attending attentive
176 dear Q4; F2 has *sweet,* which many editors adopt (the early texts are not helpful: Q1 has *Madame*—which is an unlikely address at this point, and Q2 has *My Neece,* of which the second word has been proposed as a spelling of Niesse—a young hawk that has never flown; though appropriate to the falcon metaphor for Romeo, *Niesse* seems a most unlikely, obscure, and indeed affected term for a lover to use in addressing his beloved—when Juliet speaks of Romeo as a tassel-gentle, she does not address him)
188 wanton spoiled or cruel child
190 gyves fetters

And with a silken thread plucks it back again,
So loving-jealous of his liberty.

ROMEO. I would I were thy bird.

JULIET. Sweet, so would I.
Yet I should kill thee with much cherishing.° 195
Good night, good night! Parting is such sweet sorrow
That I shall say good night till it be morrow.°

ROMEO. Sleep dwell upon thine eyes, peace in thy breast!
Would I were sleep and peace, so sweet to rest!
[*Exit Juliet.*]
Hence will I to my ghostly° father's cell, 200
His help to crave and my dear hap° to tell. *Exit.*

Enter Friar [*Laurence*] *alone, with a basket.* II iii

FRIAR. The grey-eyed morn smiles on the frowning night,
Check'ring the Eastern clouds with streaks of light;
And fleckèd° darkness like a drunkard reels
From forth day's path and Titan's fiery wheels.°
Now, ere the sun advance his burning eye 5
The day to cheer and night's dank dew to dry,°
I must up-fill this osier cage° of ours
With baleful° weeds and precious-juicèd flowers.
The earth that's nature's mother is her tomb.
What is her burying grave, that is her womb; 10
And from her womb children of divers kind
We sucking on her natural bosom find,
Many for many virtues° excellent,

195 cherishing caressing
197 morrow morning
200 ghostly spiritual
201 dear hap good fortune (but probably with an ironical glance on Shakespeare's part at *dear account*, which Romeo has forgotten: see I v 125n)
II iii 3 fleckèd i.e. with daylight
4 Titan's . . . wheels the burning wheels of the sun god's chariot
5-6 ere . . . dry all herbs were held to be most efficacious when gathered with dew on them
7 osier cage basket woven of willow branches
8 baleful poisonous
13 virtues specific efficacies

None but for some, and yet all different.
O, mickle° is the powerful grace° that lies 15
In plants, herbs, stones, and their true qualities;°
For naught so vile that on the earth doth live
But to the earth° some special good doth give;
Nor aught so good but, strained° from that fair use,
Revolts from true birth,° stumbling° on abuse. 20
Virtue itself turns vice, being misapplied,
And vice sometime's by action dignified.°

Enter Romeo [*unseen*°].

Within the infant rind° of this weak flower
Poison hath residence, and medicine power;°
For this, being smelt, with that part° cheers each part; 25
Being tasted, stays° all senses with the heart.
Two such opposèd kings encamp them still°
In man as well as herbs—grace° and rude will;
And where the worser is predominant,
Full soon the canker° death eats up that plant. 30

ROMEO. Good morrow, father.

FRIAR. Benedicite!°
What early tongue so sweet saluteth me?
Young son, it argues a distemperèd° head
So soon to bid good morrow to thy bed. 35
Care keeps his watch in every old man's eye,
And where care lodges, sleep will never lie;
But where unbruisèd° youth with unstuffed° brain
Doth couch his limbs, there golden° sleep doth reign.

---

15 **mickle** much
15 **grace** i.e. divine force
16 **qualities** properties
18 **to the earth** i.e. to earth's inhabitants
19 **strained** diverted
20 **Revolts . . . birth** turns away from its true nature
20 **stumbling** tripping over but also falling into (the drunkard image of 3-4, above, may still be in Shakespeare's mind)
22 **dignified** made worthy (i.e. a fault or wrong may sometimes in its working out bring a good result)
22 **s.d.** Qq and Ff place Romeo's entry here, possibly by error but perhaps reflecting an intended irony, as Romeo, who is to die of poison, enters with the mention of it and overhears the Friar's soliloquy about *grace* and *rude will*
23 **infant rind** tender skin
24 **medicine power** i.e. a healing property (coexisting with the poison) also has power
25 **with that part** with its odor stimulates each part of the body
26 **stays** stops
27 **still** always
28 **grace** i.e. receptiveness to divine grace
30 **canker** cankerworm
32 **Benedicite** bless you (pronounced bé-nedíssitee)
34 **distemperèd** troubled
38 **unbruisèd** not yet buffeted (by life's disappointments)
38 **unstuffed** free from cares
39 **golden** i.e. precious

Therefore thy earliness doth me assure 40
Thou art uproused with some distemp'rature;°
Or if not so, then here I hit it right—
Our Romeo hath not been in bed to-night.

ROMEO. That last is true—the sweeter rest was mine.

FRIAR. God pardon sin! Wast thou with Rosaline? 45

ROMEO. With Rosaline, my ghostly father? No.
I have forgot that name and that name's woe.

FRIAR. That's my good son! But where hast thou been then?

ROMEO. I'll tell thee ere thou ask it me again.
I have been feasting with mine enemy, 50
Where on a sudden one hath wounded me
That's by me wounded. Both our remedies
Within thy help and holy physic° lies.
I bear no hatred, blessèd man, for, lo,
My intercession° likewise steads° my foe. 55

FRIAR. Be plain, good son, and homely° in thy drift.°
Riddling confession finds but riddling shrift.°

ROMEO. Then plainly know my heart's dear love is set
On the fair daughter of rich Capulet;
As mine on hers, so hers is set on mine, 60
And all combined, save what thou must combine
By holy marriage. When, and where, and how
We met, we wooed, and made exchange of vow,
I'll tell thee as we pass; but this I pray,
That thou consent to marry us to-day. 65

FRIAR. Holy Saint Francis! What a change is here!
Is Rosaline, that thou didst love so dear,
So soon forsaken? Young men's love then lies
Not truly in their hearts, but in their eyes.
Jesu Maria! What a deal of brine 70
Hath washed thy sallow cheeks for Rosaline!
How much salt water thrown away in waste
To season° love, that of it doth not taste!°

---

41 distemp'rature i.e. unease or disease
53 physic healing power (to be expressed in marrying them)
55 intercession entreaty
55 steads helps
56 homely simple
56 drift style of speech
57 shrift absolution (but the Friar's overall meaning is that till he knows what the problem is he can't help solve it)
73 season preserve (by soaking in salt water, as meats were formerly preserved for winter) but with a pun on *season* = flavor
73 that . . . taste: has now lost its savor

The sun not yet thy sighs from heaven clears,°
Thy old groans yet ring in mine ancient ears. 75
Lo, here upon thy cheek the stain doth sit
Of an old tear that is not washed off yet.
If e'er thou wast thyself, and these woes thine,
Thou and these woes were all for Rosaline.
And art thou changed? Pronounce this sentence° then: 80
Women may fall° when there's no strength° in men.

ROMEO. Thou chid'st me oft for loving Rosaline.

FRIAR. For doting, not for loving, pupil mine.

ROMEO. And bad'st me bury love.

FRIAR. Not in a grave 85
To lay one in, another out to have.

ROMEO. I pray thee chide me not: her I love now
Doth grace for grace° and love for love allow;
The other did not so.

FRIAR. O, she knew well 90
Thy love did read by rote, that could not spell.°
But come, young waverer, come go with me.
In one respect° I'll thy assistant be;
For this alliance may so happy prove
To turn your households' rancor to pure love. 95

ROMEO. O, let us hence! I stand on° sudden haste.

FRIAR. Wisely and slow. They stumble° that run fast.

Exeunt.

Enter Benvolio and Mercutio. **II iv**

MERCUTIO. Where the devil should° this Romeo be? came he not home to-night?°

---

74 sighs . . . clears a stock humorous comparison of the lovers' sighs to clouds or mist: see I i 129-30
80 sentence maxim
81 Women may fall no wonder women are inconstant
81 strength stability
88 grace favor
91 read . . . spell i.e. recite memorized phrases rather than actually understand
93 In one respect on one consideration
96 stand on press for
97 stumble see 20, above
II iv 1 should can
2 to-night last night

BENVOLIO. Not to his father's. I spoke with his man.

MERCUTIO. Why, that same pale hard-hearted wench, that
Rosaline, torments him so that he will sure run mad. 5

BENVOLIO. Tybalt, the kinsman to old Capulet, hath sent
a letter to his father's house.

MERCUTIO. A challenge, on my life.

BENVOLIO. Romeo will answer it.°

MERCUTIO. Any man that can write may answer a letter.° 10

BENVOLIO. Nay, he will answer the letter's master, how he
dares, being dared.

MERCUTIO. Alas, poor Romeo, he is already dead! stabbed°
with a white wench's black eye; run through° the ear with
a love song; the very pin° of his heart cleft° with the blind 15
bow-boy's° butt-shaft;° and is he a man to encounter
Tybalt?°

BENVOLIO. Why, what is Tybalt?

MERCUTIO. More than Prince of Cats.° O, he's the courageous
captain of compliments.° He fights as you sing pricksong° 20
—keeps time,° distance,° and proportion;° he rests his
minim rests,° one, two, and the third in your bosom! the
very butcher of a silk button,° a duellist,° a duellist! a
gentleman of the very first house,° of the first and second
cause.° Ah, the immortal passado!° the punto reverso!° 25
the hay!°

---

9 answer it take up the challenge
10 answer a letter Mercutio pretends to misunderstand
13-15 stabbed, run through, cleft i.e. dead of three different weapons—dagger, sword, bow
15 pin the wooden pin at a target's center
16 blind bow-boy Cupid
16 butt-shaft Mercutio has his usual joke at Romeo's expense, comparing Cupid's arrow, by which his heart has supposedly been *cleft,* to a barbless practice-arrow used in shooting at the *butt* (= target)
16-17 is . . . Tybalt i.e. since he is "dead" of love already
19 Prince of Cats alluding to the cat named Tybalt or Tybert in medieval French narratives of Reynard the Fox
20 captain of compliments master of fencing
20 sing pricksong sing from written notes rather than by ear, i.e. sing with precision
21 time, distance, proportion terms relevant (1) to fencing, in the sense of timing footwork, distancing the body from the opponent, and regulating the rhythm of thrusts; and (2) to music, in the sense of tempo, intervals (of pitch), and ratio (duration of one note in relation to another)
22 minim rests in music, the shortest rests; in fencing, the pauses: i.e. he makes two feints—*one, two*—and then thrusts home *(the third in your bosom)*
23 butcher . . . button i.e. so accurate he can cut any button on his opponent's shirt
23 duellist a term brand new in England at this time like the other Italian-derived terms to follow, like the rapier itself, and like the "thrusting" style to fight it brought with it as opposed to the English sword and the "cutting" style—all these importations were fashionable and "precious," as is everything Mercutio attributes to Tybalt in this passage
24 first house school of fencing
24-25 first and second cause the two "causes" or insults calling forth a challenge

BENVOLIO. The what?°

MERCUTIO. The pox of° such antic, lisping, affecting fantasticoes—these new tuners of accent!° 'By Jesu, a very good blade! a very tall° man! a very good whore!' Why, is not 30 this a lamentable thing, grandsir,° that we should be thus afflicted with these strange flies,° these fashion-mongers, these pardon-me's,° who stand° so much on the new form° that they cannot sit at ease on the old bench? O, their bones, their bones!° 35

Enter Romeo.

BENVOLIO. Here comes Romeo! here comes Romeo!

MERCUTIO. Without his roe,° like a dried herring. O flesh, flesh, how art thou fishified!° Now is he for the numbers° that Petrarch flowed in. Laura,° to° his lady, was a kitchen wench (marry, she had a better love to berhyme her), 40 Dido° a dowdy,° Cleopatra a gypsy,° Helen° and Hero° hildings° and harlots, Thisbe° a grey eye or so, but not to the purpose.° Signior Romeo, bon jour!° There's a French

---

25-26 passado, punto reverso, hay forward lunge ("pass"), backhand thrust ("point reversed"), home thrust (hai = "I have it")—probably the three strokes noted in 22, which Mercutio doubtless reenacts here with much bowing and flourishing
27 what *Hai* is so new a term Benvolio is not familiar with it
28 The pox of "Plague take"
28-29 antic . . . accent i.e. followers of fashionable extravagances, especially in speech (if Mercutio means to parody their lisping, Shakespeare has provided him with every opportunity: "lithping . . . fantathicoeth . . . theeth new tunerth of acthenth")
30 tall brave
31 grandsir here Mercutio (whose name derives from "mercurial") may mean to drop suddenly into a typical complaint (and probably the typical cracked tone) of old men, or he may mean only to chaff Benvolio for his sedateness
32 flies butterflies
33 pardon-me's etiquette-lovers (spoken probably with a mocking foreign accent)
33 stand insist (with a glance at the literal sense in opposition to *sit)*
33 form fashion (with a pun on *form* = bench, which they cannot sit at ease on because (1) in a general sense they have given up the old sound English ways, and (2) more specially, in their new-style slim breeches the customary bare wood bench is too uncomfortable for them)
35 bones possibly with a pun on French *bon,* since the fantasticoes affect foreign phrases, and with an allusion to the bone-ache (syphilis) acquired from commerce of the sort implied in their "very good whore" (30)
37 Without his roe i.e. "a shotten herring," one that has cast its roe (here equivalent to sperm); Mercutio chooses to assume that Romeo has spent the night with Rosaline or some other
38 fishified transformed (with a glance at the usual partition of the animate creation into fish, flesh, and fowl and possibly at the frequent association of *fish* of various sorts with prostitution: see *Hamlet* II ii 187)
38 numbers verses
39 Laura beloved of Petrarch
39 to compared to
41 Dido Queen of Carthage, who loved Aeneas
41 dowdy frump
41 gypsy (1) slut (2) Egyptian
41 Helen Helen of Troy
41 Hero priestess of Aphrodite, to visit whom her lover, Leander, nightly swam the Hellespont until he was drowned in a great storm
42 hildings "good-for-nothings"
42 Thisbe beloved of Pyramus (in a story which resembles that of Romeo and Juliet and which is acted out by Bottom and his fellow craftsmen in *A Midsummer Night's Dream)*

salutation to your French slop.° You gave us the counterfeit fairly° last night. 45

ROMEO. Good morrow to you both. What counterfeit did I give you?

MERCUTIO. The slip,° sir, the slip. Can you not conceive?°

ROMEO. Pardon, good Mercutio. My business was great,° and in such a case° as mine a man may strain courtesy. 50

MERCUTIO. That's as much as to say, such a case as yours constrains a man to bow in the hams.°

ROMEO. Meaning, to curtsy.

MERCUTIO. Thou has most kindly hit it.

ROMEO. A most courteous exposition.° 55

MERCUTIO. Nay, I am the very pink° of courtesy.

ROMEO. Pink for flower.

MERCUTIO. Right.

ROMEO. Why, then is my pump well-flowered.°

MERCUTIO. Sure wit!° Follow me this jest now till thou hast worn out thy pump, that,° when the single sole of it is worn, the jest may remain, after the wearing, solely singular.° 60

42-43 not . . . purpose not worth mentioning
43 bon jour good morning
44 slop the loose breeches worn to the masquerade
45 fairly thoroughly
48 slip slang for counterfeit coin
48 conceive understand
49-52 business . . . great, case, case, bow . . . hams probably used here with an undermeaning—case (cf. modern "box") being an old term for the female sex organ
52 bow . . . hams bend at the hips (Romeo deflects Mercutio's sexual allusion—if there is one—by presuming him to refer to the simple mannerliness of a bow)
53-55 Meaning . . . exposition these lines seem to presuppose some sort of exuberant stage business now lost—does Romeo perhaps "pink" (= stab, pierce, perforate—used comically) Mercutio with his toe as he performs an elaborate curtsy in response to one by Romeo? this would give extra point to Mercutio's *Thou . . . hit it* and to Romeo's *A . . . exposition* (exposition = "exposure" as well as "interpretation") and might explain Mercutio's calling himself the *pink* of courtesy (56) as well as introduce the ensuing conversation about Romeo's "pinked" *pump* (57-61)
56 pink perfection—with allusion to pink = flower ("the flower of courtesy") and possibly to some such stage business as that noted in 53-55n
59 well-flowered i.e. well-"pinked" (perforated with an ornamental design)
60 Sure wit i.e. "What a wit you have!" (with allusion to the sure scent of a good hunting dog)
61 that so that
61-63 single sole . . . solely singular a passage of debatable meaning, in which (1) *sole* refers to the pump but perhaps also to the jest ("brevity is the *soul* of wit"); (2) *solely* may mean "with respect to sole" and "with respect to soul" as well as "altogether," "absolutely"; (3) *singular* may mean "outstanding," "precious," in addition to "odd" or "eccentric" and "single," i.e. not strong but weak; and the drift of the whole seems to be simply that a jest is quickly worn out if overworked (see *Hamlet* I iii 113)

ROMEO. O single-soled jest, solely singular for the single-ness!°

MERCUTIO. Come between us,° good Benvolio! My wits faint. 65

ROMEO. Swits and spurs,° swits and spurs! or I'll cry a match.°

MERCUTIO. Nay, if our wits run the wild-goose chase,° I am done; for thou hast more of the wild goose° in one of thy wits than, I am sure, I have in my whole five. Was I with you there° for the goose? 70

ROMEO. Thou wast never with me for anything when thou wast not there for the goose.°

MERCUTIO. I will bite thee by the ear° for that jest.

ROMEO. Nay, good goose, bite not!°

MERCUTIO. Thy wit is a very bitter sweeting;° it is a most sharp sauce.° 75

ROMEO. And is it not, then, well served in to a sweet° goose?

MERCUTIO. O, here's a wit of cheveril,° that stretches from an inch narrow to an ell° broad!

ROMEO. I stretch it out for that word 'broad,' which, added to the goose, proves thee far and wide a broad° goose. 80

MERCUTIO. Why, is not this better now than groaning for love? Now art thou sociable, now art thou Romeo; now art thou what thou art, by art as well as by nature.° For

---

64 single, single-ness Romeo plays on single = weak, silly

65 come . . . us i.e. as a third party might do to halt a fencing match

66 Swits and spurs switches and spurs, i.e. keep your horse (your wit) on the gallop

66 cry a match say I've won

67 wild-goose chase "a horse race . . . in which the second or any succeeding horse had to follow accurately the course of the leader . . . like a flight of wild geese" (OED)

68 more . . . goose i.e. more silliness

69-70 Was . . . there did I make a "hit" (i.e. in calling you a goose)

72 for the goose i.e. with your eye out for a "goose"=whore

73 bite . . . ear i.e. as one dog does another (playfully)

74 good . . . not proverbial for "spare me" (but it is not easy to see why Mercutio calls this retort a *very bitter sweeting,* i.e. a keen thrust, unless he understands Romeo to be using *goose* with one or more of its figurative meanings: simpleton, prostitute, venereal disease)

75 bitter sweeting a play on "bittersweet," the *sweeting* being "a sweet-flavored . . . apple" (OED)

76 sauce (1) relish (as apple-sauce with goose) (2) retort

77 sweet (1) applied to Mercutio as a dear friend, but also (2) to goose as a sweet (i.e. fresh, unsalted) meat

78 cheveril kid-skin, which can be stretched easily (as Romeo has stretched the meanings of "goose," making—as Mercutio implies—his little wit go a long way)

79 ell English measure of 45 inches

81 broad (1) obvious (2) indecent of speech (an attribute Mercutio proceeds to show immediately)

83-84 now . . . nature Mercutio evidently likes the chime of *art* with the two preceding *arts,* but he also makes the legitimate point that Romeo is now behaving like himself with none of the posturings of the melancholy lover

this drivelling love is like a great natural° that runs lolling° up and down to hide his bauble° in a hole. 85

BENVOLIO. Stop there, stop there!

MERCUTIO. Thou desirest me to stop in my tale against the hair.°

BENVOLIO. Thou wouldst else have made thy tale large.° 90

MERCUTIO. O, thou art deceived! I would have made it short; for I was come to the whole° depth of my tale, and meant indeed to occupy the argument° no longer.°

Enter Nurse and her Man [*Peter*].°

ROMEO. Here's goodly gear!°

MERCUTIO. A sail,° a sail! 95

BENVOLIO. Two, two! a shirt and a smock.°

NURSE. Peter!

PETER. Anon.

NURSE. My fan, Peter.

MERCUTIO. Good Peter, to hide her face; for her fan's the fairer face. 100

NURSE. God ye good morrow, gentlemen.

MERCUTIO. God ye good-den,° fair gentlewoman.°

NURSE. Is it good-den?

MERCUTIO. 'Tis no less, I tell ye; for the bawdy hand of the dial is now upon the prick° of noon. 105

---

85 natural idiot (i.e. one who shows only "nature" and none of the effects of "art" = training, education, discipline: 84)
85 lolling this probably means "with tongue hanging out" (a frequent mark of idiocy) but may refer to the dangling of his bauble
86 bauble i.e. baton of the court fool (with the obvious sexual pun)
88-89 against the hair against my inclination (*lit.* "contrary to the direction in which an animal's hair naturally lies" (OED); but again with a sexual undermeaning, as in *tale*—88, 90, 92)
90 large indecent
92 whole pun on "hole"
93 occupy the argument pursue the matter (but with pun on *occupy* = copulate)
93 no longer probably with a sexual undermeaning—see *short* in 91
93 s.d. placed as in F1; Q1 and Q2 place after 94, but it seems probable that Romeo calls attention to the Nurse's pseudo-elegance in costume and in being attended by a man-servant rather than to Mercutio's bawdy talk
94 gear "get-up" (referring to the Nurse's appearance)
95 sail alluding to the Nurse's resemblance in her finery to a ship under full canvas
96 shirt . . . smock i.e. a man and a woman
103 good-den good evening
103 fair gentlewoman ironically spoken (since it is clear the Nurse is only *affecting* to be a gentlewoman, and Mercutio at once feels her out in her own language, 105-6)
106 prick any of the marks dividing up the circumference of a clock or sun dial (here with sexual undermeaning)

NURSE. Out upon you! What a man° are you!

ROMEO. One, gentlewoman, that God hath made for himself to mar.°

NURSE. By my troth, it is well said.° 'For himself to mar,' quoth 'a?° Gentlemen, can any of you tell me where I may find the young Romeo? 110

ROMEO. I can tell you; but young Romeo will be older when you have found him than he was when you sought him. I am the youngest° of that name, for fault of a worse.° 115

NURSE. You say well.

MERCUTIO. Yea, is the worst° well? Very well took,° i' faith! wisely, wisely.

NURSE. If you be he, sir, I desire some confidence° with you.

BENVOLIO. She will endite° him to some supper. 120

MERCUTIO. A bawd,° a bawd, a bawd! So ho!°

ROMEO. What hast thou found?°

MERCUTIO. No hare,° sir; unless a hare, sir, in a lenten pie, that is something stale and hoar° ere it be spent.

[*He walks by them and sings.*]°

An old hare hoar, 125
And an old hare hoar,
Is very good meat in Lent;
But a hare that is hoar
Is too much for a score°
When it hoars ere it be spent. 130

---

107 What a man what sort of man
109 mar i.e. ruin (to *make* or *mar* is a stock proverbial antithesis)
110 By . . . said the Nurse presents herself as a connoisseur of fine phrases, not knowing that this one is a commonplace
111 quoth 'a said he
115 youngest i.e. because the only one
113-15 but . . . worse Romeo cannot resist embroidering on the Nurse's *young Romeo* in a manner calculated to confuse her, calling himself *the youngest of that name* (when he is the only one), *for fault of a worse* (when the expected statement would be *for fault*—i.e. *want*—*of a better)*
117 worst "worst" because, as Romeo has indicated, there is none *worse*
117 took understood
119 confidence a malapropism for conference
120 endite i.e. invite (Benvolio responds with a conscious malapropism)
121 A bawd Mercutio pretends to suppose that the Nurse is arranging an assignation for Romeo
121 So ho! hunter's cry upon sighting the quarry—in this case, the "hare": see 123
122 found hunter's term for discovery of game
123 hare with a pun on *hare* = whore, i.e. the Nurse is only such *meat* (see 127) as might be found *in a lenten pie,* which (because meat is forbidden during Lent) grows stale before it is consumed
124 hoar grey and moldy (with the predictable pun on "whore")
124 s.d. from Q1
129 too . . . score too inferior to justify any score, i.e. any charge for it, but possibly with some reference to the scoring of (i.e. making notches in) meat before cooking

Romeo, will you come to your father's? We'll to dinner thither.

ROMEO. I will follow you.

MERCUTIO. Farewell, ancient lady. Farewell [*sings*] lady, lady, lady.° *Exeunt* [*Mercutio, Benvolio*]. 135

NURSE. I pray you, sir, what saucy merchant° was this that was so full of his ropery?°

ROMEO. A gentleman, nurse, that loves to hear himself talk and will speak more in a minute than he will stand to° in a month. 140

NURSE. An 'a speak anything against me, I'll take him down,° an 'a were lustier than he is, and twenty such Jacks; and if I cannot, I'll find those that shall. Scurvy knave! I am none of his flirt-gills;° I am none of his skains-mates.° [*She turns to Peter, her man.*] And thou must stand by too, and 145 suffer every knave to use me at his pleasure!°

PETER. I saw no man use you at his pleasure. If I had, my weapon° should quickly have been out, I warrant you. I dare draw as soon as another man, if I see occasion in a good quarrel, and the law on my side. 150

NURSE. Now, afore God, I am so vexed that every part about me quivers. Scurvy knave! Pray you, sir, a word; and, as I told you, my young lady bid me inquire you out. What she bid me say, I will keep to myself; but first let me tell ye, if ye should lead her in a fool's paradise,° as they say, 155 it were a very gross kind of behavior, as they say; for the gentlewoman is young; and therefore, if you should deal

---

134-35 lady . . . lady refrain from a ballad, "Chaste Susanna" (with obvious reference to the Nurse's adopted air of supreme respectability
136 merchant fellow
137 ropery knavish talk
139 stand to make good on
141 An . . . down since Mercutio has said almost nothing that is not in some way insulting, this is a hilarious revelation both of how little she has understood him *(An . . . against me)* and how easily that same ignorance of language can trap her into making innuendoes about herself fully as damaging to her pose of respectability as any insults of his *(I'll . . . down):* see also *stand by,* 145; *suffer . . . pleasure,* 147; *every . . . quivers,* 151-52
144 flirt-gills flirting Jills, wenches
144 skains-mates a riddling phrase, perhaps from *skene* = knife, i.e. cut-throats' companions (modern "gun-molls")
144-45 s.d...from Q1
146 use . . . pleasure insult me (with unintended pun on *use* = have sexual intercourse with)
147-48 my weapon with again a sexual undermeaning that Peter does not grasp
155 lead . . . paradise seduce her

double with her, truly it were an ill thing° to be offered to any gentlewoman, and very weak° dealing.

ROMEO. Nurse, commend me to thy lady and mistress. I protest unto thee— 160

NURSE. Good heart, and i' faith I will tell her as much. Lord, Lord! she will be a joyful woman.

ROMEO. What will thou tell her, nurse? Thou dost not mark me.° 165

NURSE. I will tell her, sir, that you do protest, which, as I take it, is a gentlemanlike offer.

ROMEO. Bid her devise some means to come to shrift° this afternoon—and there she shall at Friar Laurence' cell be shrived and married. Here is for thy pains. 170

NURSE. No, truly, sir; not a penny.

ROMEO. Go to!° I say you shall.

NURSE. This afternoon, sir? Well, she shall be there.

ROMEO. And stay, good nurse, behind the abbey wall.
Within this hour my man shall be with thee 175
And bring thee cords made like a tackled stair,°
Which to the high topgallant° of my joy
Must be my convoy° in the secret night.
Farewell. Be trusty, and I'll quit° thy pains.
Farewell. Commend me to thy mistress. 180

NURSE. Now God in heaven bless thee! Hark you, sir.

ROMEO. What say'st thou, my dear nurse?

NURSE. Is your man secret? Did you ne'er hear say,
Two may keep counsel, putting one away?°

ROMEO. I warrant thee my man's as true as steel. 185

---

158 thing possibly, in this context, a Shakespearean quibble on thing = sex organ (not intended by the Nurse)
159 weak unmanly (the modest joke, again unintended by the Nurse, consists in the conflict of "double dealing" with "weak dealing")
164-65 mark me follow my meaning
168 shrift confession
172 Go to come, come (in her pose as gentlewoman, the Nurse affects to resist payment—but then accepts it)
176 tackled stair rope ladder
177 topgallant topmost canvas of a ship
178 convoy conveyance (but keeping the nautical image in 176-78)
179 quit reward
184 Two . . . away (1) a secret is safe with two people—if you remove one? (2) a secret is safe with two people but not three?

NURSE. Well, sir, my mistress is the sweetest lady. Lord, Lord! when 'twas a little prating thing°—O, there is a nobleman in town, one Paris, that would fain lay knife aboard;° but she, good soul, had as lieve° see a toad, a very toad, as see him. I anger her sometimes, and tell her that Paris is the properer° man; but I'll warrant you, when I say so, she looks as pale as any clout° in the versal° world. Doth not rosemary° and Romeo begin both with a letter?° 190

ROMEO. Ay, nurse; what of that? Both with an R.

NURSE. Ah, mocker! that's the dog's name.° R is for the— No; I know it begins with some other letter;° and she hath the prettiest sententious° of it, of you° and rosemary, that it would do you good to hear it. 195

ROMEO. Commend me to thy lady.

NURSE. Ay, a thousand times. [*Exit Romeo.*] Peter! 200

PETER. Anon.

NURSE. Before, and apace. *Exit* [*after Peter*].

II v

Enter Juliet.

JULIET. The clock struck nine when I did send the nurse;
In half an hour she promised to return.
Perchance she cannot meet him. That's not so.
O, she is lame! Love's heralds should be thoughts,
Which ten times faster glides° than the sun's beams 5

---

187 when . . . thing evidently the Nurse is of a mood to tell the story of Juliet's falling backwards but thinks better of it
188 lay . . . aboard get in on the feast (from the Elizabethan habit of claiming a place at table by laying out one's knife), but with a sexual undermeaning (from "boarding a vessel") that again undercuts the Nurse's pretensions
189 had as lieve would just as soon
191 properer handsomer
192 clout cloth
192 versal universal
193 rosemary an herb symbolizing remembrance
193 a letter i.e. the same letter
195 the . . . name (because r-r-r-r-is supposed to sound like a growl)
196 some . . . letter i.e. because the Nurse, who plainly cannot spell, associates "r" with the sound *ar,* with which she knows Romeo and rosemary do not begin (it has been suggested that for this reason the word she thinks to propose in 195 is *arse,* until she thinks better of it)
197 sententious she means "sentences" (i.e. wise sayings)
197 you possibly a quibble on *yew*

II v 5 glides a not uncommon Elizabethan plural form

Driving back shadows over low'ring hills.
Therefore do nimble-pinioned° doves° draw Love,
And therefore hath the wind-swift Cupid wings.
Now is the sun upon the highmost hill°
Of this day's journey, and from nine till twelve 10
Is three long hours; yet she is not come.
Had she affections° and warm youthful blood,
She would be as swift in motion as a ball;
My words would bandy° her to my sweet love,
And his to me.° 15
But old folks, many feign as they were dead°—
Unwieldy, slow, heavy and pale as lead.

Enter Nurse [and Peter].

O God, she comes! O honey nurse, what news?
Hast thou met with him? Send thy man away.

NURSE. Peter, stay at the gate. *[Exit Peter.]* 20

JULIET. Now, good sweet nurse—O Lord, why lookest thou sad?
Though news be sad, yet tell them merrily;
If good, thou shamest the music of sweet news
By playing it to me with so sour a face.

NURSE. I am aweary, give me leave° awhile. 25
Fie, how my bones ache! What a jaunce° have I!

JULIET. I would thou hadst my bones, and I thy news.
Nay, come, I pray thee speak. Good, good nurse, speak.

NURSE. Jesu, what haste! Can you not stay° awhile?
Do you not see that I am out of breath? 30

JULIET. How art thou out of breath when thou hast breath
To say to me that thou art out of breath?
The excuse that thou dost make in this delay
Is longer than the tale thou dost excuse.
Is thy news good or bad? Answer to that. 35

---

7 **nimble-pinioned** swift-winged
7 **doves** Venus's birds, which draw her chariot
9 **highmost hill** zenith (morning is conceived as a steep upward climb toward noon)
12 **affections** natural feelings
14 **bandy** bat (as a ball in tennis)
15 **his to me** his words would bat her back to me
16 **feign . . . dead** act as if they were already dead
25 **give me leave** let me be
26 **jaunce** jouncing (of my old bones)
29 **stay** wait

Say either, and I'll stay the circumstance.°
Let me be satisfied, is't good or bad?

NURSE. Well, you have made a simple° choice; you know not how to choose a man. Romeo? No, not he. Though his face be better than any man's, yet his leg excels all men's;° 40 and for a hand and a foot, and a body, though they be not to be talked on,° yet they are past compare. He is not the flower of courtesy, but, I'll warrant him, as gentle as a lamb. Go thy ways, wench; serve God. What, have you dined at home? 45

JULIET. No, no. But all this did I know before.
What says he of our marriage? What of that?

NURSE. Lord, how my head aches! What a head have I!
It beats as it would fall in twenty pieces.
My back a° t' other side°—ah, my back, my back! 50
Beshrew° your heart for sending me about
To catch my death with jauncing up and down!

JULIET. I' faith, I am sorry that thou art not well.
Sweet, sweet, sweet nurse, tell me, what says my love?

NURSE. Your love says, like an honest gentleman, 55
And a courteous, and a kind, and a handsome,
And, I warrant, a virtuous—Where is your mother?

JULIET. Where is my mother? Why, she is within.
Where should she be? How oddly thou repliest!
'Your love says, like an honest gentleman, 60
"Where is your mother?" '

NURSE. O God's Lady° dear!
Are you so hot?° Marry come up, I trow.°
Is this the poultice for my aching bones?
Henceforward do your messages yourself. 65

JULIET. Here's such a coil!° Come, what says Romeo?

NURSE. Have you got leave to go to shrift° to-day?

---

36 stay the circumstance wait for details
38 simple foolish
40 yet . . . men's probably spoken with a pause after *yet* or *leg* to make Juliet's face fall as she anticipates a criticism
41-42 not . . . on hardly worth mentioning (again the Nurse teases her, as also, for a third time, in *He . . . courtesy)*
50 a on
50 My . . . side Juliet here perhaps shows solicitude by rubbing the Nurse's back
51 Beshrew curse (spoken playfully)
62 God's Lady the Virgin Mary
63 hot angry
63 Marry . . . trow an expression of impatience ("Well, that for you!")
66 coil fuss
67 shrift confession

JULIET. I have.

NURSE. Then hie you hence to Friar Laurence' cell;
There stays a husband to make you a wife. 70
Now comes the wanton blood up in your cheeks:
They'll be in scarlet straight° at any news.
Hie you to church; I must another way,
To fetch a ladder, by the which your love
Must climb a bird's nest° soon when it is dark. 75
I am the drudge, and toil in your delight;
But you shall bear the burden soon at night.
Go; I'll to dinner; hie you to the cell.

JULIET. Hie to high fortune! Honest nurse, farewell. *Exeunt.*

Enter Friar [Laurence] and Romeo. **II vi**

FRIAR. So smile° the heavens upon this holy act
That after-hours with sorrow chide us not!

ROMEO. Amen, amen! But come what sorrow can,
It cannot countervail° the exchange of joy
That one short minute gives me in her sight. 5
Do thou but close our hands with holy words,
Then love-devouring death do what he dare°—
It is enough I may but call her mine.

FRIAR. These violent delights have violent ends
And in their triumph die, like fire and powder, 10
Which, as they kiss, consume.° The sweetest honey
Is loathsome° in his own deliciousness
And in the taste confounds° the appetite.

---

72 **straight** straightway
75 **climb . . . nest** i.e. climb to Juliet's room (with pun on bird = maiden)

II vi 1 **smile** i.e. may they smile
4 **countervail** counterbalance
7 **Then . . . dare** a challenge later taken up: see V iii 101-5
11 **consume** a triple pun compressing in one word many of the central implications of the play: (1) to be destroyed; (2) to reach a consummation, i.e. fulfillment, of what one has it in oneself to be—as the fire and powder have it in themselves to make a flash of flame and the lovers to make their deaths a triumph; (3) to consummate a marriage sexually
12 **Is loathsome** i.e. if too much is eaten
13 **confounds** destroys

Therefore love moderately: long love doth so;
Too swift arrives as tardy as too slow. 15

[*Enter Juliet somewhat fast and embraceth Romeo*]°

Here comes the lady. O, so light a foot
Will ne'er wear out° the everlasting flint.°
A lover may bestride the gossamer°
That idles in the wanton° summer air,
And yet not fall; so light is vanity. 20

JULIET. Good even to my ghostly° confessor.°

FRIAR. Romeo shall thank thee, daughter, for us both.

JULIET. As much° to him, else is his thanks too much.

ROMEO. Ah, Juliet, if the measure of thy joy
Be heaped like mine, and that° thy skill be more° 25
To blazon° it, then sweeten with thy breath
This neighbor air, and let rich music's tongue
Unfold° the imagined° happiness that both
Receive in either° by this dear° encounter.

JULIET. Conceit, more rich in matter than in words, 30
Brags of his substance, not of ornament.°

---

15 s.d. from Q1
16-17 O . . . flint a much debated passage: the Friar may mean no more than to stress the lightness of Juliet's happy step as she approaches his cell to be married ("so light a step that though they say repeated footfalls or even waterdrops will eventually wear down the hardest rock, *her* step would never do so"); alternatively, in view of 18-20, the Friar may mean to insist that there exist inexorable realities, summed up here in his enigmatic phrase *the everlasting flint*, besides which, for all its graces, romantic love appears fragile, lightweight, vain; but see also 17n
17 ne'er wear out never wear away—but with a possible phonic pun on ne'er/near and with a possible secondary meaning in *wear out* (= "outlast") that for the audience may tend to qualify the Friar's hackneyed wisdom: e.g. Juliet's light foot (with all that it signifies in the way of youth, grace, and committed love) *will* "near[ly] outlast" the everlasting flint, or even "near[ly] wear it away"
17 everlasting flint (1) life's harsh road (flint was favored for paving because of its hardness)? (2) the rigor of eternal law (whose spokesman the Friar is by profession)? (3) the stones over which (in Shakespeare's mind) Juliet perhaps walks as she comes in?
18 gossamer spiderweb
19 wanton sportive
21 ghostly spiritual
21 confessor pronounced here cónfessór
23 As much the same greeting
22-23 Romeo . . . too much possibly 22 indicates that Romeo then kisses Juliet and 23 that she returns his kiss (but nothing in the lines requires this)
25 and that and if
25 more more than mine
26 blazon publish (to blazon is (1) to describe a coat of arms heraldically (2) to catalogue in a love poem the beloved's charms)
26-28 sweeten . . . Unfold i.e. then speak of our love in that voice which to me is like music (see II ii 172-74)
28 imagined i.e. as set forth in images of what the future holds
28-29 both . . . either each receives from the other
29 dear prized (but, as so often in this play, with an undermeaning for the audience = "costly")
30-31 Conceit . . . ornament Juliet (always more direct and less self-conscious than Romeo) replies to his appeal for expression that the truest understander of an experience takes pride in its substance rather than in the ornament he might give it with words

They are but beggars that can count their worth;°
But my true love is grown to such excess
I cannot sum up sum of half my wealth.

FRIAR. Come, come with me, and we will make short work; 35
For, by your leaves, you shall not stay alone
Till Holy Church incorporate two in one. [*Exeunt.*]

Enter Mercutio, Benvolio, and [*their*] *Men.* III i

BENVOLIO. I pray thee, good Mercutio, let's retire.
The day is hot, the Capels° are abroad,
And, if we meet, we shall not 'scape a brawl,
For now, these hot days, is the mad blood stirring.

MERCUTIO. Thou art like one of these fellows that, when he 5
enters the confines of a tavern, claps me his sword upon the table and says 'God send me no need of thee!' and by the operation of the second cup draws him on the drawer,° when indeed there is no need.

BENVOLIO. Am I like such a fellow? 10

MERCUTIO. Come, come, thou art as hot a Jack° in thy mood as any in Italy; and as soon moved to be moody,° and as soon moody to be moved.°

BENVOLIO. And what to?

MERCUTIO. Nay, an there were two such,° we should have 15
none shortly, for one would kill the other. Thou! why, thou wilt quarrel with a man that hath a hair more or a hair less in his beard than thou hast. Thou wilt quarrel with a man for cracking nuts, having no other reason°

---

32 They . . . worth i.e. if I could put all my love into words *(count my worth)*, it would have to be a small amount indeed (what *beggars* might own)

III i 2 Capels pronounced Cápels (= Capulets)

8-9 draws . . . drawer draws his sword on the waiter (winedrawer)

11 Jack fellow

12 moody angry

13 moody . . . moved angry at being stirred up

15 two such two like you (Mercutio deliberately misunderstands Benvolio's *to)*

19 reason probably with a pun on *raisin* (the words were pronounced alike) since raisins and nuts were served together

but because thou hast hazel° eyes. What eye but such an eye would spy out such a quarrel? Thy head is as full of quarrels as an egg is full of meat;° and yet thy head hath been beaten as addle° as an egg for quarrelling. Thou hast quarrelled with a man for coughing in the street, because he hath wakened thy dog that hath lain asleep in the sun. Didst thou not fall out with a tailor for wearing his new doublet° before Easter?° with another for tying his new shoes with old riband?° And yet thou wilt tutor me from quarrelling! 20 25

BENVOLIO. An I were so apt to quarrel as thou art, any man should buy the fee simple° of my life for an hour and a quarter.° 30

MERCUTIO. The fee simple? O simple!°

Enter Tybalt and others.°

BENVOLIO. By my head, here come the Capulets.

MERCUTIO. By my heel,° I care not. 35

TYBALT. Follow me close, for I will speak to them.
Gentlemen, good-den. A word with one of you.

MERCUTIO. And but one word with one of us?
Couple it with something; make it a word and a blow.

TYBALT. You shall find me apt enough to that, sir, an you will give me occasion. 40

MERCUTIO. Could you not take some occasion without giving?

TYBALT. Mercutio, thou consortest with Romeo.

MERCUTIO. Consort?° What, dost thou make us minstrels? An thou make minstrels of us, look to hear nothing but 45

---

20 hazel alluding of course to hazel-nuts
22 meat i.e. contents
23 addle empty (see *full* in 22), but with a pun on *addle egg* = rotten egg
27 doublet jacket
26-27 for wearing . . . Easter (1) because he blossomed out in his spring finery before the proper date for discarding sober Lenten attire? (2) because *you* wore prematurely the spring finery he made for you? (as Mercutio is humorously engaged in inventing situations in which there is a minimum of justification for the quarrelsomeness it pleases him to attribute to Benvolio, interpretation 2 may be more satisfactory than interpretation 1)
28 riband i.e. shoe laces
31 fee simple absolute possession
31-32 for . . . quarter for the extremely low price that would be paid if the purchaser knew his ownership was to last only an hour and a quarter
33 O simple i.e. Oh how stupid (either Mercutio's usual wit fails him here or he repeats Benvolio's *fee simple* in some sense not now recoverable)
33 s.d. after "Tybalt" Q2 names "Petruchio," a Capulet kinsman or friend (I v 138), who has no lines
35 By my heel..with pun on "heal" = health, well-being, salvation
44 Consort Mercutio takes Tybalt's consort (= associate) in a more insulting sense (consort = make music with), i.e. be a *minstrel,* a hired fiddler or entertainer

discords. Here's my fiddlestick;° here's that shall make you dance. Zounds,° consort!

BENVOLIO. We talk here in the public haunt of men.
Either withdraw unto some private place,
Or reason coldly° of your grievances, 50
Or else depart.° Here all eyes gaze on us.

MERCUTIO. Men's eyes were made to look, and let them gaze.
I will not budge for no man's pleasure, I.

Enter Romeo.

TYBALT. Well, peace be with you, sir. Here comes my man.

MERCUTIO. But I'll be hanged, sir, if he wear your livery.° 55
Marry, go before to field,° he'll be your follower!°
Your worship° in that sense may call him man.

TYBALT. Romeo, the love I bear thee can afford
No better term than this: thou art a villain.°

ROMEO. Tybalt, the reason that I have to love thee° 60
Doth much excuse the appertaining rage°
To such a greeting. Villain am I none.
Therefore farewell. I see thou knowest me not.

TYBALT. Boy,° this shall not excuse the injuries
That thou hast done me; therefore turn and draw. 65

ROMEO. I do protest I never injured thee,
But love thee better than thou canst devise°
Till thou shalt know the reason of my love;
And so, good Capulet, which name I tender°
As dearly as mine own, be satisfied. 70

MERCUTIO. O calm, dishonorable, vile submission!

---

46 fiddlestick i.e. rapier
47 Zounds "by God's wounds"
50 coldly calmly
51 depart part
55 livery Mercutio also chooses to take Tybalt's word *man* in an insulting sense (= manservant)
56 field duelling field
56 follower pursuer (to fight with you), but punning on *follower* = servant (see *man:* 54, 57)
57 worship a title of honor (here sarcastic)
59 villain the term here rather means "base," "low," "no gentleman" than "wicked"
60 reason . . . thee i.e. his kinship with the Capulet family now that he is married to Juliet
61 Doth . . . rage i.e. excuses me from feeling the anger appropriate
64 Boy consciously insulting (as is his following echo of *excuse)*
67 devise imagine
69 tender hold

Alla stockado° carries it away.° [*Draws.*]
Tybalt, you ratcatcher,° will you walk?°

TYBALT. What wouldst thou have with me?

MERCUTIO. Good King of Cats, nothing but one of your nine lives. That I mean to make bold withal,° and, as you shall use me hereafter, dry-beat° the rest of the eight. Will you pluck your sword out of his pilcher° by the ears? Make haste, lest mine be about your ears ere it be out. 75

TYBALT. I am for you. [*Draws.*] 80

ROMEO. Gentle Mercutio, put thy rapier up.

MERCUTIO. Come, sir, your passado!° [*They fight.*]

ROMEO. Draw, Benvolio; beat down their weapons.
Gentlemen, for shame! forbear this outrage!
Tybalt, Mercutio, the Prince expressly hath 85
Forbid this bandying° in Verona streets.
Hold, Tybalt! Good Mercutio!

Tybalt under Romeo's arm thrusts Mercutio in° and flies.°

MERCUTIO. I am hurt.
A plague a° both your houses! I am sped.°
Is he gone and hath nothing? 90

BENVOLIO. What, art thou hurt?

MERCUTIO. Ay, ay, a scratch, a scratch. Marry, 'tis enough.
Where is my page? Go, villain,° fetch a surgeon.
[*Exit Page.*]

ROMEO. Courage, man. The hurt cannot be much.

MERCUTIO. No, 'tis not so deep as a well, nor so wide as a church door; but 'tis enough, 'twill serve. Ask for me 95

---

72 Alla stockado from *alla staccata* (an Italian fencing term = "at the thrust") which Mercutio applies as a contemptuous nickname for Tybalt, possibly with the implication that Romeo is showing timidity in the face of the new Italian style of duelling
72 carries it away wins the match
73 ratcatcher since Tybalt is King of Cats: see II iv 19n and 75
73 walk step aside with me
76 make . . . withal i.e. take
77 dry-beat thrash (but drawing no blood)
78 pilcher scabbard (*lit.* a coarse garment and therefore probably meant to be insulting, as is the suggestion that the sword would have to be plucked out by the ears, i.e. would be reluctant, i.e. Tybalt is afraid)
82 your passado i.e. "your boasted Italian lunge": see II iv 20ff and notes
86 bandying exchanging blows
87 s.d. thrusts . . . in gives Mercutio a thrust
87 s.d. from Q1; Q2 has "Away Tybalt"
89 a o' = of, i.e. on (also 98, 105)
89 sped dispatched, done for
93 villain a term applied to servants, meaning simply low-born: see above, 59n

to-morrow, and you shall find me a grave° man. I am peppered,° I warrant, for this world. A plague a both your houses! Zounds, a dog, a rat, a mouse, a cat, to scratch a man to death! a braggart, a rogue, a villain, that 100
fights by the book of arithmetic!° Why the devil came you between us? I was hurt under your arm.

ROMEO. I thought all for the best.

MERCUTIO. Help me into some house, Benvolio,
Or I shall faint. A plague a both your houses! 105
They have made worms' meat of me.
I have it,° and soundly too. Your houses!

Exit [*supported by Benvolio*].

ROMEO. This gentleman, the Prince's near ally,°
My very° friend, hath got this mortal° hurt
In my behalf—my reputation stained 110
With Tybalt's slander—Tybalt, that an hour
Hath been my cousin. O sweet Juliet,
Thy beauty hath made me effeminate
And in my temper° soft'ned valor's steel!

Enter Benvolio.

BENVOLIO. O Romeo, Romeo, brave° Mercutio is dead! 115
That gallant spirit hath aspired° the clouds,
Which too untimely° here did scorn the earth.

ROMEO. This day's black fate on moe° days doth depend;°
This but begins the woe others must end.

[*Enter Tybalt.*]

BENVOLIO. Here comes the furious Tybalt back again. 120

---

97 grave (1) sobered (2) buried (in a grave)
97-98 I am peppered I've had my death blows (*pepper*—OED 5); but probably with a pun on "peppering" as a phase in the dressing of meat (i.e. "I'm as done for in this world as meat that is already killed and dressed": see *worms' meat* in 106); and conceivably, Mercutio being the incorrigible wag that he is, with a further pun on being *peppered* = infected with a venereal disease (OED 7)
101 by . . . arithmetic i.e. by precise adherence to fencing-school rules
107 I . . . it perhaps a touching echo of the *hay* in II iv 26
108 ally kinsman
109 very true
109 mortal deathly
114 temper disposition (but the image is of a sword blade which has failed to be properly *tempered* = hardened, or, alternatively, whose *temper* has failed)
115 brave noble
116 aspired risen to
117 untimely prematurely (i.e. while still a young man)
118 moe more
118 depend hang over (i.e. Mercutio's death hangs a cloud over things to come)

ROMEO. Alive in triumph, and Mercutio slain?
Away to heaven respective° lenity,°
And fire-eyed fury° be my conduct° now!
Now, Tybalt, take the 'villain' back again
That late thou gavest me; for Mercutio's soul 125
Is but a little way above our heads,
Staying° for thine to keep him company.
Either thou or I, or both, must go with him.

TYBALT. Thou, wretched boy, that didst consort him here,
Shalt with him hence. 130

ROMEO. This° shall determine that. *They fight. Tybalt falls.*

BENVOLIO. Romeo, away, be gone!
The citizens are up,° and Tybalt slain.
Stand not amazed.° The Prince will doom thee death
If thou art taken. Hence, be gone, away! 135

ROMEO. O, I am fortune's fool!°

BENVOLIO. Why dost thou stay? *Exit Romeo.*

Enter Citizens.

CITIZEN. Which way ran he that killed Mercutio?
Tybalt, that murderer, which way ran he?

BENVOLIO. There lies that Tybalt. 140

CITIZEN. Up, sir, go with me.
I charge thee in the Prince's name obey.

Enter Prince [*attended*], *old Montague, Capulet, their Wives, and all.*

PRINCE. Where are the vile beginners of this fray?

BENVOLIO. O noble Prince, I can discover° all
The unlucky manage° of this fatal brawl. 145
There lies the man, slain by young Romeo,
That slew thy kinsman, brave Mercutio.

---

122 respective (1) merciful (2) having respect to the situation, e.g. Tybalt's kinship to Juliet
122 lenity softness
123 fire-eyed fury raving anger (personified, like *respective lenity,* to stress the moment of Romeo's choosing between them)
123 conduct guide
127 Staying waiting
131 This (as he draws his sword)
133 up up in arms
134 amazed stupefied
136 fool (1) dupe (2) court jester (in the sense of serving Fortune for mockery and laughter, as the jester does the king)
144 discover reveal
145 manage management (but with allusion to *manège,* the management of a horse: the brawl is thus represented as a steed out of control)

LADY CAPULET. Tybalt, my cousin! O my brother's child!
O Prince! O husband! O, the blood is spilled
Of my dear kinsman! Prince, as thou art true, 150
For blood of ours shed blood of Montague.
O cousin, cousin!

PRINCE. Benvolio, who began this bloody fray?

BENVOLIO. Tybalt, here slain, whom Romeo's hand did slay.
Romeo, that spoke him fair, bid him bethink 155
How nice° the quarrel was, and urged withal°
Your high displeasure. All this—utterèd
With gentle breath, calm look, knees humbly bowed—
Could not take° truce with the unruly spleen°
Of Tybalt deaf to peace, but that he tilts° 160
With piercing steel at bold Mercutio's breast;°
Who, all as hot, turns deadly point to point,
And, with a martial scorn, with one hand beats
Cold death aside and with the other° sends
It back to Tybalt, whose dexterity 165
Retorts it. Romeo he cries aloud,
'Hold, friends! friends, part!' and swifter than his tongue,
His agile arm beats down their fatal points,
And 'twixt them rushes;° underneath whose arm
An envious° thrust from Tybalt hit the life 170
Of stout° Mercutio, and then Tybalt fled;
But by and by comes back to Romeo,
Who had but newly entertained° revenge,
And to't they go like lightning; for, ere I
Could draw to part them, was stout Tybalt slain; 175
And, as he fell, did Romeo turn and fly.
This is the truth, or let Benvolio die.

LADY CAPULET. He is a kinsman to the Montague;
Affection makes him false, he speaks not true.

---

156 nice trifling
156 withal at the same time
159 take make
159 spleen quarrelsomeness
160-61 Of . . . breast Benvolio omits to mention that Mercutio forced Tybalt to fight with him
160 tilts thrusts
163-64 one hand . . . the other with dagger in the left hand, rapier in the right
169 rushes i.e. *he* rushes (not his arm)
170 envious malicious
171 stout valiant
173 entertained given thought to

Some twenty of them fought in this black strife, 180
And all those twenty could but kill one life.
I beg for justice, which thou, Prince, must give.
Romeo slew Tybalt; Romeo must not live.

PRINCE. Romeo slew him; he slew Mercutio.
Who now the price of his dear blood doth owe? 185

MONTAGUE. Not Romeo, Prince; he was Mercutio's friend;
His fault concludes but what the law should end,
The life of Tybalt.

PRINCE. And for that offense
Immediately we do exile him hence. 190
I have an interest in your hate's proceeding,
My blood° for your rude brawls doth lie a-bleeding;
But I'll amerce° you with so strong a fine
That you shall all repent the loss of mine.
I will be deaf to pleading and excuses; 195
Nor tears nor prayers shall purchase out° abuses.
Therefore use none. Let Romeo hence in haste,
Else, when he is found, that hour is his last.
Bear hence this body, and attend our will.°
Mercy but murders, pardoning those that kill. 200
Exit [with others].

Enter Juliet alone. III ii

JULIET. Gallop apace, you fiery-footed steeds,
Towards Phoebus' lodging!° Such a wagoner
As Phaëton would whip you to the west
And bring in cloudy night immediately.°
Spread thy close curtain, love-performing night, 5

---

192 My blood i.e. my kinsman (Mercutio)
193 amerce penalize
196 purchase out redeem
199 attend our will await our verdict

III ii 2 lodging i.e. the Western resting place of the sun god Phoebus, whose steeds Juliet exhorts to hurry in order that the night may come
4 immediately because when Phoebus's son Phaeton undertook to drive his father's horses they ran away with him

That runaways'° eyes may wink, and Romeo
Leap to these arms untalked of and unseen.
Lovers can see to do their amorous rites
By their own beauties; or, if love° be blind,
It best agrees with night. Come, civil° night, 10
Thou sober-suited matron, all in black,
And learn me how to lose a winning match,
Played for a pair of stainless maidenhoods.
Hood° my unmanned° blood, bating° in my cheeks,
With thy black mantle till strange° love, grown bold, 15
Think true love acted simple modesty.
Come, night; come, Romeo; come, thou day in night;
For thou wilt lie upon the wings of night
Whiter than new snow upon a raven's back.
Come, gentle night; come, loving, black-browed night; 20
Give me my Romeo; and, when he shall die,
Take him and cut him out in little stars,
And he will make the face of heaven so fine
That all the world will be in love with night
And pay no worship to the garish° sun. 25
O, I have bought the mansion of a love,
But not possessed it; and though I am sold,
Not yet enjoyed.° So tedious is this day
As is the night before some festival
To an impatient child that hath new robes 30
And may not wear them. O, here comes my nurse,

Enter Nurse, with cords.°

---

6 runaways' perhaps the sun's horses, here wishfully thought of by Juliet as again running away to the West in order that their eyes may soon close *(wink)* and day disappear; or perhaps, with emendation to "runaway," merely the roving eyes of men, the expression having been influenced by the Phaeton image above (this word constitutes one of the best-known textual problems in Shakespeare and has been variously interpreted to refer to nighttime vagabonds, to Juliet herself, and to night (personified) as well as variously emended to "Rumour's," "rude day's," "curious," "cunningest," etc.)
9 love i.e. blind Cupid
10 civil restrained, decorous (i.e. behaving in ways suited both to a matron and to married love considered as the foundation of "civil" life)
14 Hood i.e. cover with a black hood (as a falcon's eyes were hooded by the falconer to calm it)
14 unmanned a term from falconry meaning untrained to the presence of a man, but with a pun on man = husband
14 bating again an allusion to falconry—"to beat the wings impatiently and flutter away from the perch" (OED)
15 strange shy, inexperienced
25 garish glaring
26-28 O . . . enjoyed Juliet's image begins with herself as purchaser, but shifts abruptly to herself as the house purchased
31 s.d. Q1 has *Enter Nurse wringing her hands, with the ladder of cords in her lap;* this can only mean that in the performances that Q1 records (see Textual Note) the Nurse was "discovered" at rear stage, sitting

And she brings news; and every tongue that speaks
But Romeo's name speaks heavenly eloquence.
Now, nurse, what news? What hast thou there, 35
The cords that Romeo bid thee fetch?

NURSE. Ay, ay, the cords. [*Throws them down.*]

JULIET. Ay me! what news? Why dost thou wring thy hands?

NURSE.° Ah, weraday!° he's dead, he's dead, he's dead!
We are undone, lady, we are undone!
Alack the day! he's gone, he's killed, he's dead! 40

JULIET. Can heaven be so envious?

NURSE. Romeo can,
Though heaven cannot. O Romeo, Romeo!
Who ever would have thought it? Romeo!

JULIET. What devil art thou that dost torment me thus? 45
This torture should be roared in dismal hell.
Hath Romeo slain himself? Say thou but 'I,'°
And that bare vowel 'I' shall poison more
Than the death-darting eye of cockatrice.°
I am not I, if there be such an 'I'° 50
Or those eyes shut° that makes° thee answer 'I.'
If he be slain, say 'I'; or if not, 'no.'
Brief sounds determine my weal or woe.

NURSE. I saw the wound, I saw it with mine eyes,
(God save the mark!°) here on his manly breast. 55
A piteous corse,° a bloody piteous corse;
Pale, pale as ashes, all bedaubed in blood,
All in gore-blood.° I swounded° at the sight.

JULIET. O break, my heart! poor bankrout,° break at once!
To prison, eyes; ne'er look on liberty! 60

---

38 Nurse Shakespeare keeps the outbreak of feeling in this passage at a comic distance from us through the cross-current of misunderstanding
38 weraday i.e. welladay = alas
47-52 I Juliet puns on "ay" = yes and on "eye" and "eyes" (since Elizabethan "ay" was regularly written as "I," Juliet calls it *that bare vowel*, 48)
49 cockatrice basilisk, a fabulous creature whose glance was fatal
50 such an "I" such an "ay" as that which answers yes to the question: Is Romeo dead?
51 shut i.e. in death
51 makes common Elizabethan plural: see II v 5
55 God . . . mark apologetic phrase for mentioning something unpleasant
56 corse corpse
58 gore-blood clotted blood
58 swounded swooned
59 bankrout bankrupt (with a matching pun on *break* = go bankrupt)

Vile earth,° to earth resign;° end motion° here,°
And thou and Romeo press one heavy bier!

NURSE. O Tybalt, Tybalt, the best friend I had!
O courteous Tybalt! honest gentleman!
That ever I should live to see thee dead! 65

JULIET. What storm is this that blows so contrary?
Is Romeo slaught'red, and is Tybalt dead?
My dearest cousin, and my dearer lord?
Then, dreadful trumpet,° sound the general doom!
For who is living, if those two are gone? 70

NURSE. Tybalt is gone, and Romeo banishèd;
Romeo that killed him, he is banishèd.

JULIET. O God! Did Romeo's hand shed Tybalt's blood?

NURSE. It did, it did! alas the day, it did!

JULIET. O serpent heart, hid with a flow'ring face!° 75
Did ever dragon keep so fair a cave?
Beautiful tyrant! fiend angelical!°
Dove-feathered raven! wolvish-ravening° lamb!
Despisèd substance of divinest show!°
Just° opposite to what thou justly° seem'st— 80
A damnèd saint, an honorable villain!
O nature, what hadst thou to do in hell
When thou didst bower the spirit of a fiend
In mortal paradise of such sweet flesh?°
Was ever book containing such vile matter° 85
So fairly bound? O, that deceit should dwell
In such a gorgeous palace!°

---

61 Vile earth (she refers to her own body)
61 resign yield, return
61 motion (1) movement (2) feeling
61 here presumably indicating her heart
69 dreadful trumpet the trumpet announcing Doomsday
75 with . . . face the serpent tempting Eve in Eden was often depicted thus
77-87 Beautiful . . . palace Shakespeare undertakes to capture Juliet's conflicting feelings in the conflicting language of paradox: see I i 173ff
77 fiend angelical perhaps echoing the language of 2 Corinthians 11:14, where Satan is said to disguise himself as "an angel of light"
78 wolvish-ravening again echoing the language of the Bible (Matthew 7:15) about false prophets in sheep's clothing, who inwardly "are ravening wolves"
79 substance/show reality/appearance
80 Just precisely
80 justly truly
83-84 bower . . . flesh shelter a fiend in such a handsome exterior as Romeo's (but with obvious references to Satan's presence in the paradise of Eden)
85 matter content

NURSE. There's no trust, no faith, no honesty in men;
All perjured, all forsworn, all naught,° all dissemblers.
Ah, were's my man? Give me some aqua vitae.° 90
These griefs, these woes, these sorrows make me old.
Shame come to Romeo!

JULIET. Blistered be thy tongue°
For such a wish! He was not born to shame.
Upon his brow shame is ashamed to sit; 95
For 'tis a throne where honor may be crowned
Sole monarch of the universal earth.
O, what a beast was I to chide at him!

NURSE. Will you speak well of him that killed your cousin?

JULIET. Shall I speak ill of him that is my husband? 100
Ah, poor my lord, what tongue shall smooth thy name
When I, thy three-hours wife, have mangled it?
But wherefore, villain, didst thou kill my cousin?
That villain cousin would have killed my husband.
Back, foolish tears, back to your native spring! 105
Your tributary° drops belong to woe,
Which you, mistaking, offer up to joy.°
My husband lives, that Tybalt would have slain;
And Tybalt's dead, that would have slain my husband.
All this is comfort; wherefore weep I then? 110
Some word there was, worser than Tybalt's death,
That murd'red me. I would forget it fain;
But O, it presses to my memory
Like damnèd guilty deeds to sinners' minds!
'Tybalt is dead, and Romeo—banishèd.' 115
That 'banishèd,' that one word 'banishèd,'
Hath slain° ten thousand Tybalts. Tybalt's death
Was woe enough, if it had ended there;
Or, if sour woe delights in fellowship
And needly will be ranked° with other griefs, 120
Why followèd not, when she said 'Tybalt's dead,'

---

89 naught wicked
90 aqua vitae alcoholic spirits
93 Blistered . . . tongue a punishment for slander
106 tributary (1) offered as tribute (2) flowing like a tributary stream into a larger stream or ocean (in this case, *woe*)
107 to joy i.e. on an occasion that actually calls fo joy since Romeo is not dead
117 Hath slain is worse than hearing of the death of
120 needly . . . ranked insists on being accompanied

Thy father, or thy mother, nay, or both,
Which modern° lamentation might have moved?
But with a rearward° following Tybalt's death,
'Romeo is banishèd'—to speak that word 125
Is father, mother, Tybalt, Romeo, Juliet,
All slain, all dead. 'Romeo is banishèd'—
There is no end, no limit, measure, bound,
In that word's death;° no words can that woe sound.°
Where is my father and my mother, nurse? 130

NURSE. Weeping and wailing over Tybalt's corse.
Will you go to them? I will bring you thither.

JULIET. Wash they his wounds with tears? Mine shall be spent,
When theirs are dry, for Romeo's banishment.
Take up those cords. Poor ropes, you are beguiled,° 135
Both you and I, for Romeo is exiled.
He made you for a highway to my bed;
But I, a maid, die maiden-widowèd.
Come, cords; come, nurse. I'll to my wedding bed;
And death, not Romeo, take my maidenhead! 140

NURSE. Hie to your chamber. I'll find Romeo
To comfort you. I wot° well where he is.
Hark ye, your Romeo will be here at night.
I'll to him; he is hid at Laurence' cell.

JULIET. O, find him! give this ring to my true knight 145
And bid him come to take his last farewell.

Exit [*with Nurse*].

---

123 modern commonplace
124 rearward rearguard (perhaps with a pun on "rear word," i.e. coming at the end)
129 that . . . death the death inflicted by that word
129 sound take the depth of (as one *sounds* the depth of an ocean or stream)
135 beguiled cheated
142 wot know

Enter Friar [Laurence].° III iii

FRIAR. Romeo, come forth; come forth, thou fearful° man.
Affliction is enamored of thy parts,°
And thou art wedded to calamity.

Enter Romeo.

ROMEO. Father, what news? What is the Prince's doom?°
What sorrow craves acquaintance at my hand 5
That I yet know not?

FRIAR. Too familiar
Is my dear son with such sour° company.
I bring thee tidings of the Prince's doom.

ROMEO. What less than doomsday° is the Prince's doom? 10

FRIAR. A gentler judgment vanished° from his lips—
Not body's death, but body's banishment.

ROMEO. Ha, banishment? Be merciful, say 'death';
For exile hath more terror in his look,
Much more than death. Do not say 'banishment.' 15

FRIAR. Hence from Verona art thou banishèd.
Be patient, for the world is broad and wide.

ROMEO. There is no world without Verona walls,
But purgatory, torture, hell itself.
Hence banishèd is banished from the world, 20
And world's exile° is death. Then 'banishèd'
Is death mistermed. Calling death 'banishèd,'
Thou cut'st my head off with a golden axe
And smilest upon the stroke that murders me.

FRIAR. O deadly sin! O rude unthankfulness! 25
Thy fault our law calls death; but the kind Prince,
Taking thy part, hath rushed° aside the law,
And turned that black word 'death' to banishment.
This is dear mercy, and thou seest it not.

III iii s.d. from Q1; Q2 has *Enter Friar and Romeo*
1 fearful frightened
2 parts qualities
4 doom judgment
8 sour bitter
10 doomsday i.e. death
11 vanished i.e. issued (as a breath into the air)
21 world's exile exile from the world
27 rushed pushed

ROMEO. 'Tis torture, and not mercy. Heaven is here, 30
Where Juliet lives; and every cat and dog
And little mouse, every unworthy thing,
Live here in heaven and may look on her;
But Romeo may not. More validity,°
More honorable state,° more courtship° lives 35
In carrion flies° than Romeo. They may seize
On the white wonder of dear Juliet's hand
And steal immortal blessing from her lips,
Who,° even in pure and vestal° modesty,
Still blush, as thinking their own kisses sin;° 40
But Romeo may not, he is banishèd.
Flies may do this but I from this must fly;
They are freemen,° but I am banishèd.
And sayest thou yet that exile is not death?
Hadst thou no poison mixed, no sharp-ground knife, 45
No sudden mean° of death, though ne'er so mean,°
But 'banishèd' to kill me—'banishèd'?
O friar, the damnèd use that word in hell;
Howling attends° it! How hast thou the heart,
Being a divine, a ghostly confessor,° 50
A sin-absolver, and my friend professed,
To mangle me with that word 'banishèd'?

FRIAR. Thou fond° mad man, hear me a little speak.

ROMEO. O, thou wilt speak again of banishment.

FRIAR. I'll give thee armor to keep off that word; 55
Adversity's sweet milk, philosophy,
To comfort° thee, though thou art banishèd.

ROMEO. Yet 'banishèd'? Hang up° philosophy!
Unless philosophy can make a Juliet,

---

34 validity value
35 state privilege of rank
35 courtship i.e. opportunity for wooing (with possibly a pun on courtship = the splendid way of life appertaining to a court gathered about a king or queen, as for Romeo, all things are gathered about Juliet)
36 carrion flies flies that live on carrion
39 Who Juliet's lips
39 vestal virginal
40 their . . . sin their own touching sinful
43 freeman i.e. like men who have been given "the freedom of the city"
46 mean means
46 mean lowly
49 attends accompanies
50 confessor pronounced cónfessór
53 fond foolish
57 comfort i.e. sustain (as food)
58 Hang up i.e. like obsolete armor (see 55)

Displant a town,° reverse a prince's doom, 60
It helps not, it prevails not. Talk no more.

FRIAR. O, then I see that madmen have no ears.

ROMEO. How should they, when that wise men have no eyes?

FRIAR. Let me dispute° with thee of thy estate.°

ROMEO. Thou canst not speak of that thou dost not feel. 65
Wert thou as young as I, Juliet thy love,
An hour but married, Tybalt murderèd,
Doting like me, and like me banishèd,
Then mightst thou speak:
Then mightst thou tear thy hair,° 70
And fall upon the ground, as I do now,
Taking the measure° of an unmade grave.
[*Knocking within*].°

FRIAR. Arise; one knocks. Good Romeo, hide thyself.

ROMEO. Not I; unless the breath of heartsick groans
Mist-like° infold me from the search of eyes. [*Knock.*] 75

FRIAR. Hark, how they knock! Who's there? Romeo, arise;
Thou wilt be taken.—Stay awhile!—Stand up; *Loud Knock*
Run to my study.—By and by!°—God's will,°
What simpleness° is this.—I come, I come! *Knock.*
Who knocks so hard? Whence come you? What's your will? 80

Enter Nurse.

NURSE. Let me come in, and you shall know my errand.
I come from Lady Juliet.

FRIAR. Welcome then.

NURSE. O holy friar, O, tell me, holy friar,
Where is my lady's lord, where's Romeo? 85

---

60 Displant a town i.e. move Verona with Juliet in it
64 dispute reason
64 estate situation
69-70 Then . . . hair printed as one line in Q1 and most editions; but Q2's separation into two lines gives an emphasis to Romeo's retort *(Thou canst not speak,* 65; *Then mightst thou speak,* 70) that is worth preserving
72 Taking the measure i.e. with my prostrate body
72, 75, 77, 79: s.d. Q2 has, respectively: *Enter Nurse and knock; They knock; slud* [loud? still?] *knock;* and *knock.* But Q2 also has *Enter Nurse* after l. 80, as here
75 Mist-like see the language used about sighs at I i 129
78 By and by i.e. coming immediately
78 God's will i.e. God's will be done (but with the effect of a mild oath: "in God's name")
79 simpleness foolishness (that Romeo will not hide)

FRIAR. There on the ground, with his own tears made drunk.

NURSE.° O, he is even in my mistress' case,
Just in her case! O woeful sympathy!
Piteous predicament! Even so lies she,
Blubb'ring and weeping, weeping and blubb'ring. 90
Stand up, stand up! Stand, an you be a man.
For Juliet's sake, for her sake, rise and stand!
Why should you fall into so deep an O?°

ROMEO. [*rises*] Nurse—

NURSE. Ah sir! ah sir! Death's the end of all. 95

ROMEO. Spakest thou of Juliet? How is it with her?
Doth not she think me an old° murderer,
Now I have stained the childhood of our joy
With blood removed but little from her own?
Where is she? and how doth she! and what says 100
My concealed lady° to our cancelled° love?

NURSE. O, she says nothing, sir, but weeps and weeps;
And now falls on her bed, and then starts up,
And Tybalt calls; and then on° Romeo cries,
And then down falls again. 105

ROMEO. As if that name,
Shot from the deadly level° of a gun,
Did murder her; as that name's cursèd hand°
Murdered her kinsman. O, tell me, friar, tell me,
In what vile part of this anatomy° 110
Doth my name lodge? Tell me, that I may sack
The hateful mansion.°

[*He offers to stab himself, and Nurse snatches the dagger away.*]°

87-93 Nurse Shakespeare again insists on comic distance by placing bawdy innuendoes in the Nurse's talk that are quite unrealized by her—as in *case* (see II iv 49-52n), *stand, rise, O*
93 an O i.e. a groan
97 old hardened
101 concealed lady secret wife (pronounced here cóncealed to jingle with *cancelled)*
101 cancelled annulled (by my banishment)
104 on against
107 level line of aim
108 that . . . hand i.e. the cursed hand belonging to the man of that name
110 anatomy bodily frame
111-12 sack . . . mansion destroy that part of me where my name lies (for *mansion*, see III ii 26)
112 s.d. from Q1

FRIAR. Hold thy desperate hand.
Art thou a man? Thy form cries out thou art;
Thy tears are womanish, thy wild acts denote 115
The unreasonable° fury of a beast.
Unseemly° woman in a seeming° man!
And ill-beseeming beast in seeming both!°
Thou hast amazed me. By my holy order,
I thought thy disposition better tempered.° 120
Hast thou slain Tybalt? Wilt thou slay thyself?
And slay thy lady that in thy life lives,
By doing damnèd° hate upon thyself?
Why railest thou on thy birth, the heaven, and earth?
Since birth and heaven and earth, all three do meet° 125
In thee at once; which thou at once wouldst lose.
Fie, fie, thou shamest thy shape, thy love, thy wit,°
Which,° like a usurer,° abound'st in all,
And usest none in that true use indeed
Which should bedeck° thy shape, thy love, thy wit. 130
Thy noble shape is but a form of wax°,
Digressing from° the valor of a man;
Thy dear love sworn° but hollow perjury,
Killing° that love which thou hast vowed to cherish;
Thy wit, that ornament to shape and love, 135
Misshapen° in the conduct° of them both,
Like powder in a skilless soldier's flask,°
Is set afire by thine own ignorance,
And thou dismemb'red with thine own defense.°

---

116 unreasonable irrational
117 Unseemly (1) incongruous (2) not seemly (i.e. not attractive to behold)
117 seeming apparent
118 ill . . . both (1) becoming less than human (i.e. a *beast*)—and an ungainly beast at that (*ill-beseeming*)? (2) inappropriate even for a beast in seeming simultaneously male and female?
120 better tempered better balanced (as among the four elements held to compose it in Renaissance physiology: see I i 137n)
123 damnèd because for suicide one was damned: see *Hamlet* I ii 133-34
125 meet i.e. the soul (from *heaven*) and the body (of *earth*) are conjoined at *birth*
127 wit reason
128 Which i.e. thou who
128 like a usurer because the usurer puts what he has to bad use (i.e. the gaining of interest on money, frowned on by Renaissance moralists and theologians)
130 bedeck be an ornament or honor to
131 a . . . wax i.e. a lifeless effigy: see I iii 78n
132 Digressing from i.e. when it fails to show
133 sworn modifies *love*
134 Killing if you kill
136 Misshapen i.e. misguided (evidently used for the jingle with *shape* 127, 130, 131, 135)
136 conduct management
137 flask powder horn
139 dismemb'red . . . defense destroyed by the very intellect that ought to protect you, as the soldier is *dismembered* by the powder intended to protect *him*

What, rouse thee, man! Thy Juliet is alive, 140
For whose dear sake thou wast but lately dead.°
There art thou happy.° Tybalt would kill thee,
But thou slewest Tybalt. There art thou happy.
The law, that threat'ned death, becomes thy friend
And turns it to exile. There art thou happy. 145
A pack of blessings light upon thy back;
Happiness° courts thee in her best array;
But, like a misbehaved and sullen wench,
Thou pouts° upon thy fortune and thy love.
Take heed, take heed, for such die miserable. 150
Go get thee to thy love, as was decreed,°
Ascend her chamber, hence and comfort her.
But look thou stay not till the watch be set,°
For then thou canst not pass to Mantua,
Where thou shalt live till we can find a time 155
To blaze° your marriage, reconcile your friends,°
Beg pardon of the Prince, and call thee back
With twenty hundred thousand times more joy
Than thou went'st forth in lamentation.
Go before, nurse. Commend me to thy lady, 160
And bid her hasten all the house to bed,
Which heavy sorrow makes them apt unto.°
Romeo is coming.

NURSE. O Lord, I could have stayed here all the night
To hear good counsel. O, what learning is! 165
My lord, I'll tell my lady you will come.

ROMEO. Do so, and bid my sweet prepare to chide.
[*Nurse offers to go in and turns again.*]°

NURSE. Here, sir, a ring she bid me give you, sir.
Hie you, make haste, for it grows very late. [*Exit.*]°

ROMEO. How well my comfort is revived by this! 170

---

141 dead i.e. calling yourself dead
142, 143, 145 happy well off
147 Happiness good fortune
149 pouts common Elizabethan second person singular
151 decreed intended
153 till . . . set (when the town- gate would also be closed)
156 blaze proclaim
156 friends kinsmen
162 apt unto inclined to
167 s.d. from Q1 (*offers to go in* = starts to go off stage)
169 s.d. from Q1

FRIAR. Go hence; good night; and here stands all your state:°
Either be gone before the watch be set,
Or by the break of day disguised from hence.
Sojourn in Mantua. I'll find out your man,°
And he shall signify from time to time 175
Every good hap to you that chances here.
Give me thy hand. 'Tis late. Farewell; good night.

ROMEO. But that a joy past joy calls out on me,
It were a grief so brief to part with thee.
Farewell. *Exeunt.* 180

Enter old Capulet, his Wife, and Paris. III iv

CAPULET. Things have fall'n out, sir, so unluckily
That we have had no time to move° our daughter.
Look you, she loved her kinsman Tybalt dearly,
And so did I. Well, we were born to die.
'Tis very late; she'll not come down to-night. 5
I promise° you, but for your company,
I would have been abed an hour ago.

PARIS. These times of woe afford no times to woo.
Madam, good night. Commend me to your daughter.

LADY CAPULET. I will, and know her mind early to-morrow; 10
To-night she's mewed up to her heaviness.°
[*Paris offers to go in, and Capulet calls him again.*]°

CAPULET. Sir Paris, I will make a desperate tender°
Of my child's love. I think she will be ruled
In all respects by me; nay more, I doubt it not.
Wife, go you to her ere you go to bed; 15

---

171 here . . . state i.e. your whole future depends on your doing as follows
174 man servant

III iv 2 move i.e. speak about your suit with
6 promise assure
11 mewed . . . heaviness caged up (like a falcon when moulting) in her grief
11 s.d. from Q1
12 desperate tender reckless offer (he has no way of knowing *how* reckless, since at his last acquaintance with Juliet's feelings (I iii) they were malleable)

Acquaint her here° of my son° Paris' love
And bid her (mark you me?) on Wednesday next—
But soft! what day is this?

PARIS. Monday, my lord.

CAPULET. Monday! ha, ha!° Well, Wednesday is too soon. 20
A° Thursday let it be—a Thursday, tell her,
She shall be married to this noble earl.
Will you be ready? Do you like this haste?
We'll keep no great ado—a friend or two;
For hark you, Tybalt being slain so late, 25
It may be thought we held him carelessly,
Being our kinsman, if we revel much.
Therefore we'll have some half a dozen friends,
And there an end. But what say you to Thursday?

PARIS. My lord, I would that Thursday were to-morrow. 30

CAPULET. Well, get you gone. A Thursday be it then.
Go you to Juliet ere you go to bed;
Prepare her, wife, against° this wedding day.
Farewell, my lord.—Light to my chamber, ho!
Afore me,° it is so very late 35
That we may call it early by and by.°
Good night. *Exeunt.*

Enter Romeo and Juliet aloft [at the window].° III v

JULIET. Wilt thou be gone? It is not yet near day.
It was the nightingale, and not the lark,
That pierced the fearful° hollow of thine ear.
Nightly she sings on yond pomegranate tree.
Believe me, love, it was the nightingale. 5

---

16 here i.e. without delay (here at this moment of time)
16 son i.e. intended son-in-law
20 ha, ha probably more indicators of hesitation like "h'm"
21 A of (= on)
33 against for
35 Afore me a mild oath ("God before me") approximating "upon my word"
36 by and by i.e. almost at once

III v I s.d. from Q1 except *aloft*, which is from Q2
3 fearful apprehensive

ROMEO. It was the lark, the herald of the morn;
No nightingale. Look, love, what envious° streaks
Do lace° the severing° clouds in yonder East.
Night's candles° are burnt out, and jocund° day
Stands tiptoe on the misty mountain tops. 10
I must be gone and live, or stay and die.

JULIET. Yond light is not daylight; I know it, I.
It is some meteor that the sun exhales°
To be to thee this night a torchbearer
And light thee on thy way to Mantua. 15
Therefore stay yet; thou need'st not to be gone.

ROMEO. Let me be ta'en, let me be put to death.
I am content, so thou wilt have it so.
I'll say yon grey is not the morning's eye,
'Tis but the pale reflex of Cynthia's brow;° 20
Nor that is not the lark whose notes do beat
The vaulty° heaven so high above our heads.
I have more care° to stay than will to go.
Come, death, and welcome! Juliet wills it so.
How is't, my soul?° Let's talk; it is not day. 25

JULIET. It is, it is! Hie hence, be gone, away!
It is the lark that sings so out of tune,
Straining harsh discords and unpleasing sharps.
Some say the lark makes sweet division;°
This doth not so, for she divideth us. 30
Some say the lark and loathèd toad changed° eyes;
O, now I would they had changed voices too,
Since arm from arm that voice doth us affray,°
Hunting° thee hence with hunt's-up° to the day.
O, now be gone! More light and light it grows. 35

---

7 **envious** i.e. of the lovers' joy (and therefore terminating it with daylight)
8 **lace** make lacy patterns on (but with a further play on *lace* = fasten together as antithesis to *severing*)
8 **severing** separating from each other
9 **Night's candles** the stars
9 **jocund** merry
13 **It . . . exhales** "luminous meteors" and "fiery meteors" were thought to result from the ignition of gases exhaled by the sky or a heavenly body
20 **reflex . . . brow** the moon's reflection
22 **vaulty** vaulted
23 **care** desire
25 **my soul** i.e. Juliet
29 **division** harmonious modulation of notes (with pun on *division* = separation)
31 **changed** exchanged (alluding to a folk saying that, since the eyes of the toad are large and luminous and those of the lark small, the two must have exchanged eyes)
33 **affray** frighten
34 **Hunting** i.e. chasing
34 **hunt's up** a song or cry to awaken huntsmen (but also used for those newly married)

ROMEO. More light and light—more dark and dark our woes.

Enter Nurse [hastily].

NURSE. Madam!

JULIET. Nurse?

NURSE. Your lady mother is coming to your chamber.
The day is broke; be wary, look about. [*Exit.*] 40

JULIET. Then, window, let day in, and let life out.

ROMEO. Farewell, farewell! One kiss, and I'll descend.
[*He goeth down.*]°

JULIET. Art thou gone so? Love, lord, ay husband, friend°—
I must hear from thee every day in the hour,
For in a minute there are many days. 45
O, by this count° I shall be much° in years
Ere I again behold my Romeo!

ROMEO. Farewell!
I will omit° no opportunity
That may convey my greetings, love, to thee. 50

JULIET. O, think'st thou we shall ever meet again?

ROMEO. I doubt it not; and all these woes shall serve
For sweet discourses in our times to come.

JULIET. O God, I have an ill-divining° soul!
Methinks I see thee, now thou art so low, 55
As one dead in the bottom of a tomb.
Either my eyesight fails, or thou lookest pale.

ROMEO. And trust me, love, in my eye so do you.
Dry° sorrow drinks our blood. Adieu, adieu! *Exit.*

JULIET. O Fortune, Fortune! all men call thee fickle. 60
If thou art fickle, what dost thou with him°
That is renowned for faith? Be fickle, Fortune,
For then I hope thou wilt not keep him long
But send him back. [*She goeth down from the window.*]°

Enter Mother.

---

42 s.d. from Q1
43 friend common Elizabethan term for lover
46 this count this way of counting
46 much much advanced
49 omit neglect
54 ill-divining foreseeing misfortune
59 Dry thirsty (sorrow was thought to use up blood—hence, says Romeo, they are both pale)
61 what . . . him why do you keep company with him
64 s.d. from Q1

LADY CAPULET. Ho, daughter! are you up? 65

JULIET. Who is't that calls? It is my lady mother.
Is she not down° so late, or up so early?
What unaccustomed cause procures her hither?

LADY CAPULET. Why, how now, Juliet?°

JULIET. Madam, I am not well. 70

LADY CAPULET. Evermore weeping for your cousin's death?
What, wilt thou wash him from his grave with tears?
An if thou couldst, thou couldst not make him live.
Therefore have done. Some grief shows much of love;
But much of grief shows still° some want of wit. 75

JULIET. Yet let me weep for such a feeling° loss.

LADY CAPULET. So shall you feel the loss, but not the friend°
Which you weep for.

JULIET. Feeling so the loss,
I cannot choose but ever weep the friend. 80

LADY CAPULET. Well, girl, thou weep'st not so much for his death
As that the villain lives which slaughtered him.

JULIET. What villain, madam?

LADY CAPULET. That same villain Romeo.

JULIET. [*aside*] Villain and he be many miles asunder.— 85

God pardon him! I do, with all my heart;
And yet no man like° he doth grieve my heart.°

LADY CAPULET. That is because the traitor murderer lives.

JULIET. Ay, madam, from the reach of these my hands.
Would none but I might venge my cousin's death!° 90

LADY CAPULET. We will have vengeance for it, fear thou not.
Then weep no more. I'll send to one in Mantua,
Where that same banished runagate° doth live,
Shall give him such an unaccustomed dram°

---

67 **down** abed
69 **Why . . . Juliet** Lady Capulet is taken aback by Juliet's appearance
75 **still** always
76 **feeling** heartfelt
77, 80 **friend** Lady Capulet uses this term in the sense of kinsman, Juliet in the sense of lover (see 43)
87 **like** so much as
87 **grieve my heart** (1) by being absent (in Juliet's sense) (2) by being the killer of Tybalt (in Lady Capulet's)
89-90 **my . . . death** again Juliet has one meaning, her mother supposes another
93 **runagate** renegade
94 **dram** dose (of poison)

That he shall soon keep Tybalt company; 95
And then I hope thou wilt be satisfied.

JULIET. Indeed I never shall be satisfied
With Romeo till I behold him—dead°—
Is my poor heart so for a kinsman vexed.
Madam, if you could find out but a man 100
To bear a poison, I would temper° it;
That Romeo should, upon receipt thereof,
Soon sleep° in quiet. O, how my heart abhors
To hear him named and cannot° come to him,
To wreak° the love I bore my cousin 105
Upon his body that hath slaughtered him!

LADY CAPULET. Find thou the means,° and I'll find such a man.
But now I'll tell thee joyful tidings, girl.

JULIET. And joy comes well in such a needy time.
What are they, beseech your ladyship? 110

LADY CAPULET. Well, well, thou hast a careful° father, child;
One who, to put thee from thy heaviness,°
Hath sorted° out a sudden° day of joy
That thou expects° not nor I looked not for.

JULIET. Madam, in happy time!° What day is that? 115

LADY CAPULET. Marry,° my child, early next Thursday morn
The gallant, young, and noble gentleman,
The County Paris, at Saint Peter's Church,
Shall happily make thee there a joyful bride.

JULIET. Now by Saint Peter's Church, and Peter too, 120
He shall not make me there a joyful bride!
I wonder at this haste, that I must wed
Ere he that should be husband comes to woo.
I pray you tell my lord and father, madam,
I will not marry yet; and when I do, I swear 125
It shall be Romeo, whom you know I hate,
Rather than Paris. These are news indeed!

---

98 dead for Juliet this applies to "heart"; for her mother, to "Romeo"
101 temper (1) concoct (2) moderate
103 sleep (1) in death (2) in my embrace
104 and cannot when I cannot
105 wreak (1) avenge (2) give expression to
107 means i.e. the poison
111 careful considerate of your welfare
112 heaviness grief
113 sorted selected
113 sudden unexpected
114 expects common Elizabethan second person singular
115 in . . . time i.e. how opportune
116 Marry (see above I i 35n)

LADY CAPULET. Here comes your father. Tell him so yourself,
And see how he will take it at your hands.

CAPULET. When the sun sets the earth° doth drizzle dew, 130
But for the sunset of my brother's son
It rains downright.
How now? a conduit,° girl? What, still in tears?
Evermore show'ring? In one little body
Thou counterfeits° a bark,° a sea, a wind: 135
For still thy eyes, which I may call the sea,
Do ebb and flow with tears; the bark thy body is,
Sailing in this salt flood; the winds, thy sighs,
Who,° raging with thy tears and they with them,
Without a sudden° calm will overset 140
Thy tempest-tossèd body. How now, wife?
Have you deliverèd to her our decree?°

LADY CAPULET. Ay, sir; but she will none, she gives you thanks.°
I would the fool were married to her grave!

CAPULET. Soft! take me with you,° take me with you, wife. 145
How? Will she none? Doth she not give us thanks?
Is she not proud? Doth she not count her blest,
Unworthy as she is, that we have wrought°
So worthy a gentleman to be her bride?°

JULIET. Not proud you have, but thankful that you have. 150
Proud can I never be of what I hate,
But thankful even for hate that is meant love.

CAPULET. How, how, how, how, chopped-logic?° What is this?
'Proud'—and 'I thank you'—and 'I thank you not'—
And yet 'not proud'? Mistress minion° you, 155

---

130 earth emended by some editors to "air" (Q4) to improve the meteorology, but the implied comparison seems sounder and more plausible with the Q2 reading (*earth* is to *dew* as Juliet is to tears)
133 conduit fountain
135 Thou counterfeits you play the parts of (see also 114n)
135 bark ship
139 Who which
140 sudden immediate
142 Have . . . decree Capulet has come a long way since his "desperate tender" at III iv 12: he now speaks like royalty
143 give . . . thanks says no thank you
145 Soft . . . you hold on—let me understand you
148 wrought procured
149 bride bridegroom—OED 2 (but the Q2 compositor may simply have dropped groom by accident)
153 chopped-logic the phrase seems capable of interpretation either as a form of address ("What's that you're saying, my dear Lady Hairsplitter") or as a description of what Juliet has said: ("So all you have to offer is hair-splitting, eh?"), but the former is obviously more dramatic
155 minion darling ("you brat of a spoiled darling you")

Thank me no thankings, nor proud me no prouds,
But fettle your fine joints° 'gainst Thursday next
To go with Paris to Saint Peter's Church,
Or I will drag thee on a hurdle° thither.
Out, you green-sickness° carrion! out, you baggage!° 160
You tallow-face!°

LADY CAPULET. Fie, fie! what, are you mad?°

JULIET. Good father, I beseech you on my knees,
[*She kneels down.*]°
Hear me with patience but to speak a word.

CAPULET. Hang thee, young baggage! disobedient wretch! 165
I tell thee what—get thee to church a Thursday
Or never after look me in the face.
Speak not, reply not, do not answer me!
My fingers itch. Wife, we scarce thought us blest
That God had lent us but this only child; 170
But now I see this one is one too much,
And that we have a curse in having her.
Out on her, hilding!°

NURSE. God in heaven bless her!
You are to blame, my lord, to rate° her so. 175

CAPULET. And why, my Lady Wisdom? Hold your tongue,
Good Prudence. Smatter with your gossips,° go!

NURSE. I speak no treason.

CAPULET. O, God-i-god-en!°

NURSE. May not one speak? 180

CAPULET. Peace, you mumbling° fool!
Utter your gravity o'er a gossip's bowl,
For here we need it not.

---

157 fettle . . . joints make ready (but perhaps with a slight glance at *fettle* = to groom a horse; or, alternatively, at *joints* = meat divided and dressed for consumption)
159 hurdle sledge for dragging criminals to execution
160 green-sickness anemic (see II ii 8n): Juliet has grown pale
160 baggage good-for-nothing woman
161 tallow-face i.e. pale as tallow
162 Fie . . . mad addressed to Capulet
163 s.d. from Q1
173 hilding good-for-nothing
175 rate berate
177 Smatter . . . gossips chatter with your cronies (see II i 13n)
179 God-i-god-en God give you good evening (but here spoken with elaborate sarcastic deference as if from a servant to a superior)
181 mumbling a taunt at the Nurse's lack of teeth (see I iii 14-15 and *mumble*, OED 3: "to chew . . . softly, as with toothless gums")

LADY CAPULET. You are too hot.°

CAPULET. God's bread!° it makes me mad.° 185
Day, night, hour, tide, time, work, play;
Alone, in company—still° my care hath been
To have her matched; and having now provided
A gentleman of noble parentage,
Of fair demesnes,° youthful, and nobly trained, 190
Stuffed, as they say, with honorable parts,
Proportioned as one's thought would wish a man—
And then to have a wretched puling° fool,
A whining mammet,° in her fortune's tender,°
To answer 'I'll not wed, I cannot love; 195
I am too young, I pray you pardon me'!
But, an you will not wed, I'll pardon you!°
Graze where you will, you shall not house with me.
Look to't, think on't; I do not use° to jest.
Thursday is near; lay hand on heart,° advise:° 200
An you be mine, I'll give you to my friend;
An you be not, hang, beg, starve, die in the streets,
For, by my soul, I'll ne'er acknowledge thee,
Nor what is mine shall never do thee good.
Trust to't.° Bethink you. I'll not be forsworn.° *Exit.* 205

JULIET. Is there no pity sitting in the clouds
That sees into the bottom of my grief?
O sweet my mother, cast me not away!
Delay this marriage for a month, a week;
Or if you do not, make the bridal bed 210
In that dim monument where Tybalt lies.

LADY CAPULET. Talk not to me, for I'll not speak a word.°
Do as thou wilt, for I have done with thee. *Exit.*

---

184 hot agitated
185 God's bread i.e. "by the bread of the Sacrament"
185 makes me mad drives me crazy
187 still always
190 demesnes domains
193 puling whining
194 mammet puppet (spoken with contempt)
194 in . . . tender i.e. when fortune is offered her
197 pardon you i.e. dismiss you forever
199 do not use am not accustomed
200 lay . . . heart take the matter seriously
200 advise consider
205 Trust to't i.e. you can rely on it
205 be foresworn break my oath
212 word i.e. on your behalf

JULIET. O God!—O nurse, how shall this be prevented?
My husband is on earth, my faith in heaven.° 215
How shall that faith return again to earth°
Unless that husband send it me from heaven
By leaving earth?° Comfort me, counsel me.
Alack, alack, that heaven should practise strategems
Upon so soft a subject as myself! 220
What say'st thou? Hast thou not a word of joy?
Some comfort, nurse.

NURSE. Faith, here it is.
Romeo is banished; and all the world to nothing
That he dares ne'er come back to challenge you; 225
Or if he do, it needs must be by stealth.
Then, since the case so stands as now it doth,
I think it best you married with the County.
O, he's a lovely gentleman!
Romeo's a dishclout° to him. An eagle, madam, 230
Hath not so green,° so quick, so fair an eye
As Paris hath. Beshrew° my very heart,
I think you are happy in this second match,
For it excels your first; or if it did not,
Your first is dead—or 'twere as good he were 235
As living here and you no use of him.

JULIET. Speak'st thou from thy heart?

NURSE. And from my soul too; else beshrew them both.

JULIET. Amen!°

NURSE. What? 240

JULIET. Well, thou has comforted me marvellous much.
Go in; and tell my lady I am gone,
Having displeased my father, to Laurence' cell,
To make confession and to be absolved.

NURSE. Marry, I will; and this is wisely done. [*Exit.*] 245

---

215 my . . . heaven my marriage vow is recorded in heaven
216 return . . . earth i.e. to be reassigned to Paris
218 By . . . earth i.e. by his death
230 dishclout dishcloth
231 green an eye-color much admired by Elizabethans
232 Beshrew curse (a light oath)
239 Amen i.e. so be it

JULIET. [*She looks after Nurse.*]° Ancient damnation!°
O most wicked fiend!
Is it more sin to wish me thus forsworn,°
Or to dispraise my lord with that same tongue
Which she hath praised him with above compare
So many thousand times? Go, counsellor! 250
Thou and my bosom° henceforth shall be twain.°
I'll to the friar to know his remedy.
If all else fail, myself have power to die. *Exit.*

Enter Friar [Laurence] and County Paris. IV i

FRIAR. On Thursday, sir? The time is very short.

PARIS. My father° Capulet will have it so,
And I am nothing slow° to slack his haste.

FRIAR. You say you do not know the lady's mind.
Uneven is the course;° I like it not. 5

PARIS. Immoderately she weeps for Tybalt's death,
And therefore have I little talked of love;
For Venus smiles not° in a house of tears.
Now, sir, her father counts it dangerous
That she do give her sorrow so much sway, 10
And in his wisdow hastes our marriage
To stop the inundation of her tears,
Which, too much minded° by herself alone,
May be put from her by society.
Now do you know the reason of this haste. 15

---

246 s.d. from Q1
246 Ancient damnation damnable old woman (but possibly with a glance in *ancient* and *fiend* at a connection between the Nurse and "the Old One," the Devil)
247 forsworn guilty of breaking my oath
251 bosom confidence, trust
251 twain separated

IV i 2 father i.e. future father-in-law
3 nothing slow most unwilling (*lit.* not at all disposed to delay and by my delaying delay him)
5 Uneven . . . course the course of action that you propose is irregular
8 Venus . . . not i.e. love makes no headway (but alluding also to the astrological principle that the planet Venus cannot *smile,* i.e. exercise a benign influence when it is seen in a *house of tears,* i.e. a moist zodiacal house such as (e.g.) Aquarius
13 minded on her mind

FRIAR. [*aside*] I would I knew not why it should be slowed.
Look, sir, here comes the lady toward my cell.

Enter Juliet.

PARIS. Happily met, my lady and my wife!

JULIET. That may be, sir, when I may be a wife.

PARIS. That 'may be' must be, love, on Thursday next. 20

JULIET. What must be shall be.

FRIAR. That's a certain text.

PARIS. Come you to make confession to this father?

JULIET. To answer that, I should confess to you.

PARIS. Do not deny to him that you love me. 25

JULIET. I will confess to you that I love him.

PARIS. So will ye, I am sure, that you love me.

JULIET. If I do so, it will be of more price,
Being spoke behind your back, than to your face.

PARIS. Poor soul, thy face is much abused with tears. 30

JULIET. The tears have got small victory by that,
For it was bad enough before their spite.°

PARIS. Thou wrong'st it more than tears with that report.

JULIET. That is no slander, sir, which is a truth;
And what I spake, I spake it to my face.° 35

PARIS. Thy face is mine, and thou hast sland'red it.

JULIET. It may be so, for it is not mine own.°
Are you at leisure, holy father, now,
Or shall I come to you at evening mass?°

FRIAR. My leisure serves me, pensive daughter, now. 40
My lord, we must entreat the time alone.

PARIS. God shield° I should disturb devotion!
Juliet, on Thursday early will I rouse ye.
Till then, adieu, and keep this holy kiss. *Exit.*

---

32 spite injurious effect
35 to my face i.e. not behind my back (see 29) but openly—as *truth* should be and *slander* would not be (see 34)
37 not mine own i.e. it is Romeo's
39 evening mass prohibited but not unknown in the time of Shakespeare (who may, however, have meant simply vespers)
42 shield forbid

JULIET. O, shut the door! and when thou hast done so, 45
Come weep with me—past hope, past cure, past help!

FRIAR. Ah, Juliet, I already know thy grief;
It strains me past the compass° of my wits.
I hear thou must, and nothing may prorogue° it,
On Thursday next be married to this County. 50

JULIET. Tell me not, friar, that thou hearest of this,
Unless thou tell me how I may prevent it.
If in thy wisdom thou canst give no help,
Do thou but call my resolution wise
And with this knife I'll help it presently.° 55
God joined my heart and Romeo's, thou our hands;
And ere this hand, by thee to Romeo's sealed,
Shall be the label° to another deed,°
Or my true heart with treacherous revolt
Turn to another, this° shall slay them both. 60
Therefore, out of thy long-experienced time,°
Give me some present counsel; or, behold,
'Twixt my extremes° and me this bloody° knife
Shall play the umpire, arbitrating that
Which the commission of thy years and art° 65
Could to no issue of true honor° bring.
Be not so long to speak. I long to die
If what thou speak'st speak not of remedy.

FRIAR. Hold, daughter. I do spy a kind of hope,
Which craves as desperate an execution 70
As that is desperate which we would prevent.
If, rather than to marry County Paris,
Thou hast the strength of will to slay thyself,
Then is it likely thou wilt undertake
A thing like death to chide away this shame, 75
That cop'st° with death himself to scape from it;
And, if thou darest, I'll give thee remedy.

---

48 compass (1) limits (OED 1) (2) cunning (OED 2)
49 prorogue postpone
55 presently immediately
58 label "a narrow strip of material attached to a document to carry the seal" (OED 6)
58 deed action (with pun on *deed* = document = Juliet's and Romeo's marriage thought of in its legal aspect)
60 this see 55 above
61 time age
63 extremes difficulties
63 bloody i.e. capable of blood
65 commission . . . art authority vested in you by your years and sagacity
66 no . . . honor no honorable outcome
76 That cop'st i.e. since you are willing to cope

JULIET. O, bid me leap, rather than marry Paris,
From off the battlements of any tower,
Or walk in thievish° ways, or bid me lurk 80
Where serpents are; chain me with roaring bears,
Or hide me nightly in a charnel house,°
O'ercovered quite with dead men's rattling bones,
With reeky° shanks and yellow chapless° skulls;
Or bid me go into a new-made grave 85
And hide me with a dead man in his shroud—
Things that, to hear them told, have made me tremble—
And I will do it without fear or doubt,
To live an unstained wife to my sweet love.

FRIAR. Hold, then. Go home, be merry, give consent 90
To marry Paris. Wednesday is to-morrow.
To-morrow night look that thou lie alone;
Let not the nurse lie with thee in thy chamber.
Take thou this vial, being then in bed,
And this distilling° liquor drink thou off; 95
When presently through all thy veins shall run
A cold and drowsy° humor;° for no pulse
Shall keep his native progress,° but surcease;°
No warmth, no breath, shall testify thou livest;
The roses in thy lips and cheeks shall fade 100
To wanny° ashes, thy eyes' windows° fall
Like death when he shuts up the day of life;
Each part, deprived of supple government,°
Shall, stiff and stark and cold, appear like death;
And in this borrowed likeness of shrunk death 105
Thou shalt continue two-and-forty hours,
And then awake as from a pleasant sleep.
Now, when the bridegroom in the morning comes
To rouse thee from thy bed, there art thou dead.
Then, as the manner of our country is, 110

---

80 thievish i.e. frequented by thieves
82 charnel house depository for old bones unearthed when digging new graves
84 reeky reeking, odorous
84 chapless jawless
95 distilling permeating
97 drowsy soporific
97 humor moisture
97-98 for . . . surcease i.e. circulation of the blood will be suspended
98 native progress natural course through the body
101 wanny wan, pale (the image being of waning coals as well as fading roses)
101 eyes' windows eyelids
103 government control

In thy best robes uncovered° on the bier
Thou shalt be borne to that same ancient vault
Where all the kindred of the Capulets lie.
In the mean time, against° thou shalt awake,
Shall Romeo by my letters know our drift;° 115
And hither shall he come; and he and I
Will watch thy waking, and that very night
Shall Romeo bear thee hence to Mantua.
And this shall free thee from this present shame,
If no inconstant toy° nor womanish fear 120
Abate thy valor in the acting it.

JULIET. Give me, give me! O, tell not me of fear!

FRIAR. Hold! Get you gone, be strong and prosperous
In this resolve. I'll send a friar with speed
To Mantua, with my letters to thy lord. 125

JULIET. Love give me strength! and strength shall help afford.
Farewell, dear father. *Exit [with Friar].*

Enter Capulet, Lady Capulet, Nurse, and Servingmen, two or three. IV ii

CAPULET. So many guests invite as here are writ.
[Exit a Servingman.]
Sirrah, go hire me twenty cunning° cooks.

SERVINGMAN. You shall have none ill, sir; for I'll try° if they can lick their fingers.

CAPULET. How canst thou try them so? 5

111 uncovered with head uncovered
114 against in preparation for the time when
115 drift plan
120 toy unreasoning aversion (OED 4b)
IV ii 2 cunning knowledgeable (in cookery)
3 try test

SERVINGMAN. Marry, sir, 'tis an ill cook that cannot lick his own fingers.° Therefore he that cannot lick his fingers goes not with me.

CAPULET. Go, begone. [*Exit Servingman.*]
We shall be much unfurnished° for this time. 10
What, is my daughter gone to Friar Laurence?

NURSE. Ay, forsooth.

CAPULET. Well, he may chance to do some good on her.
A peevish self-willed harlotry° it° is.

Enter Juliet.

NURSE. See where she comes from shrift with merry look. 15

CAPULET. How now, my headstrong? Where have you been gadding?

JULIET. Where I have learnt me to repent the sin
Of disobedient opposition
To you and your behests, and am enjoined
By holy Laurence to fall prostrate here [*She kneels down.*]° 20
To beg your pardon. Pardon, I beseech you!
Henceforward I am ever ruled by you.

CAPULET. Send for the County. Go tell him of this.
I'll have this knot knit up to-morrow° morning.

JULIET. I met the youthful lord at Laurence' cell 25
And gave him what becomèd° love I might,
Not stepping o'er the bounds of modesty.

CAPULET. Why, I am glad on't. This is well. Stand up.
This is as't should be. Let me see the County.
Ay, marry, go, I say, and fetch him hither. 30
Now, afore God,° this reverend holy friar,
All our whole city is much bound° to him.

JULIET. Nurse, will you go with me into my closet°
To help me sort° such needful ornaments
As you think fit to furnish me to-morrow? 35

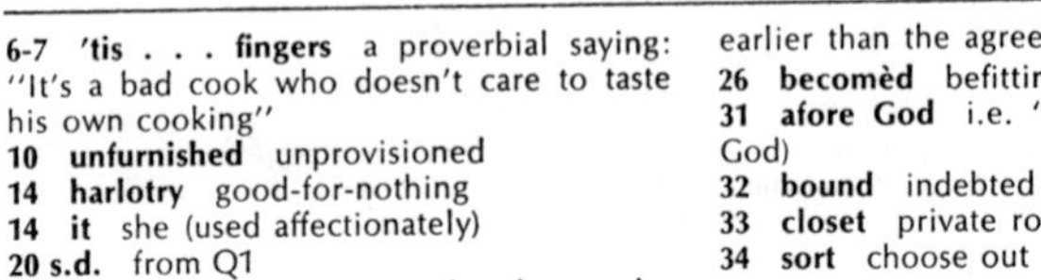

6-7 'tis . . . fingers a proverbial saying: "It's a bad cook who doesn't care to taste his own cooking"
10 unfurnished unprovisioned
14 harlotry good-for-nothing
14 it she (used affectionately)
20 s.d. from Q1
24 to-morrow i.e. on Wednesday, a day earlier than the agreement at III iv 17-22
26 becomèd befitting
31 afore God i.e. "on my word" (before God)
32 bound indebted
33 closet private room
34 sort choose out

LADY CAPULET. No, not till Thursday. There is time enough.

CAPULET. Go, nurse, go with her. We'll to church to-morrow.
Exeunt [Juliet and Nurse].

LADY CAPULET. We shall be short in our provision.
'Tis now near night.

CAPULET. Tush, I will stir about, 40
And all things shall be well, I warrant thee, wife.
Go thou to Juliet, help to deck up her.
I'll not to bed to-night; let me alone.
I'll play the housewife for this once. What, ho!
They are all forth; well, I will walk myself 45
To County Paris, to prepare up him
Against to-morrow. My heart is wondrous light,
Since this same wayward girl is so reclaimed.
Exit [with Mother].

Enter Juliet and Nurse. **IV iii**

JULIET. Ay, those attires are best; but, gentle nurse,
I pray thee leave me to myself to-night;
For I have need of many orisons°
To move the heavens to smile upon my state,°
Which, well thou knowest, is cross° and full of sin. 5

Enter Mother.

LADY CAPULET. What, are you busy, ho? Need you my help?

JULIET. No, madam; we have culled° such necessaries
As are behoveful° for our state° to-morrow.
So please you, let me now be left alone,
And let the nurse this night sit up with you; 10
For I am sure you have your hands full all
In this so sudden business.

IV iii 3 orisons prayers
4 state spiritual condition
5 cross contrary (to what it should be)
7 culled picked
8 behoveful appropriate
8 state ceremony

LADY CAPULET. Good night.
Get thee to bed, and rest; for thou hast need.
Exeunt [*Mother and Nurse*].

JULIET. Farewell! God knows when we shall meet again. 15
I have a faint cold fear° thrills through my veins
That almost freezes up the heat of life.
I'll call them back again to comfort me.
Nurse!—What should she do here?
My dismal scene I needs must act alone. 20
Come, vial.
What if this mixture do not work at all?
Shall I be married then to-morrow morning?
No, no! This shall forbid it. Lie thou there.
[*Lays down a dagger.*]
What if it be a poison which the friar 25
Subtly hath minist'red° to have me dead,
Lest in this marriage he should be dishonored
Because he married me before to Romeo?
I fear it is; and yet methinks it should not,
For he hath still° been tried° a holy man. 30
How if, when I am laid into the tomb,
I wake before the time that Romeo
Come to redeem me? There's a fearful point!
Shall I not then be stifled in the vault,
To whose foul mouth no healthsome air breathes in, 35
And there die strangled ere my Romeo comes?
Or, if I live, is it not very like
The horrible conceit° of death and night,
Together with the terror of the place—
As in a vault,° an ancient receptacle 40
Where for this many hundred years the bones
Of all my buried ancestors are packed;
Where bloody Tybalt, yet but green° in earth,
Lies fest'ring in his shroud; where, as they say,

---

16 faint . . . fear a fear that makes me feel faint and cold
26 minist'red provided (with allusion perhaps to a friar's more proper function in ministering healing or the sacraments)
30 still always
30 tried proved
38 conceit consciousness
39-40 terror . . . vault i.e. terror because I shall be locked up in a burial vault
43 green recently (but not without a shuddering overtone from *green* as the color of dead and *fest'ring* flesh)

At some hours in the night spirits resort— 45
Alack, alack, is it not like that I,
So early waking—what with loathsome smells,
And shrieks like mandrakes° torn out of the earth,
That living mortals, hearing them, run mad—
O, if I wake, shall I not be distraught,° 50
Environèd with all these hideous fears,
And madly play with my forefathers' joints,
And pluck the mangled Tybalt from his shroud,
And, in this rage, with some great kinsman's bone
As with a club dash out my desp'rate brains? 55
O, look! methinks I see my cousin's ghost
Seeking out Romeo, that did spit his body
Upon a rapier's point. Stay, Tybalt, stay!
Romeo, I come! this do I drink to thee.

[*She falls upon her bed within the curtains.*]°

Enter Lady of the House and Nurse. IV iv

LADY CAPULET. Hold, take these keys and fetch more spices, nurse.

NURSE. They call for dates and quinces in the pastry.°

Enter old Capulet.

CAPULET. Come, stir, stir, stir! The second cock hath crowed,
The curfew bell° hath rung, 'tis three o'clock.
Look to the baked meats,° good Angelica;° 5
Spare not for cost.

NURSE. Go, you cot-quean,° go,
Get you to bed! Faith, you'll be sick to-morrow
For this night's watching.°

---

48 mandrakes a plant thought to look like a human body because of its forked root and fabled to shriek so hideously when pulled from the ground that hearers ran mad
50 distraught driven insane
59 s.d. from Q1

IV iv 2 pastry pastry room
4 curfew bell i.e. the bell signaling the end of curfew
5 baked meats meat pies
5 Angelica i.e. the Nurse (who answers, and for whom this name has ironic point), not Lady Capulet
7 cot-quean a man who meddles with household duties
9 watching staying awake

CAPULET. No, not a whit. What, I have watched ere now 10
All night for lesser cause, and ne'er been sick.

LADY CAPULET. Ay, you have been a mouse-hunt° in your time;
But I will watch° you from such watching now.
Exit Lady and Nurse.

CAPULET. A jealous hood,° a jealous hood!

Enter three or four [Fellows] with spits and logs and baskets.

Now, fellow, what is there? 15

1. FELLOW. Things for the cook, sir; but I know not what.

CAPULET. Make haste, make haste. [*Exit first Fellow.*] Sirrah, fetch drier logs.
Call Peter; he will show thee where they are.

2. FELLOW. I have a head, sir, that will find out logs°
And never trouble Peter for the matter. 20

CAPULET. Mass,° and well said; a merry whoreson,° ha!
Thou shalt be loggerhead.° [*Exit second Fellow, with the others.*] Good Father!° 'tis day.
The County will be here with music straight,
For so he said he would. *Play music.* I hear him near.
Nurse! Wife! What, ho! What, nurse, I say! 25

Enter Nurse.

Go waken Juliet; go and trim° her up.
I'll go and chat with Paris. Hie, make haste,
Make haste! The bridegroom he is come already:
Make haste, I say. [*Exit.*]

---

12 mouse-hunt prowler for women
13 watch keep you under surveillance (but probably with a pun on *watch* in falconry = to prevent (a hawk) from sleeping in order to tame it—OED 8)
14 jealous hood various interpreted to mean "jealous woman" (*hood* = a type of female headdress—OED 9), "jealous spy" (*hood* = a disguise), "jealous ninny" (*hood* = *hud* = an empty person), "jealousy (*hood* = the suffix indicating generality, as in manhood, knighthood), etc.; (since hood may also = the kind of head-covering that blinds, as in falconry, the point of Capulet's playful retort to his wife's threat, likewise drawn from falconry, may simply be that in seeking to *watch* him—keep a close eye upon him against the possibility of his womanizing—she is herself showing that she is blinded by jealousy: she may "*watch*" but she can't "see")
19 that . . . logs because, being wooden like the logs, it will be drawn to them
21 Mass by the Mass
21 whoreson bastard (spoken jovially)
22 loggerhead blockhead
23 Father perhaps part of a mild oath (many editors emend to Q4's "faith," but this gains little)
26 trim dress

[*Nurse approaches Juliet's curtained bed.*] IV v

NURSE. Mistress! what, mistress! Juliet! Fast,° I warrant her,
she.
Why, lamb! why, lady! Fie, you slug-abed.°
Why, love, I say! madam! sweetheart! Why, bride!
What, not a word? You take° your pennyworths° now;
Sleep for a week; for the next night, I warrant, 5
The County Paris hath set up his rest°
That you shall rest but little. God forgive me!°
Marry, and amen. How sound is she asleep!
I needs must wake her. Madam, madam, madam!
Ay, let the County take° you in your bed; 10
He'll fright you up, i' faith. Will it not be?°
[*Draws aside the curtains.*]
What, dressed, and in your clothes, and down° again?
I must needs wake you. Lady! lady! lady! [*Shakes her.*]
Alas, alas!° Help, help! my lady's dead!
O weraday° that ever I was born! 15
Some aqua vitae,° ho! My lord! my lady!

[*Enter Mother.*]

LADY CAPULET. What noise is here?

NURSE. O lamentable day!

LADY CAPULET. What is the matter?

NURSE. Look, look! O heavy day! 20

IV v 1 Fast fast asleep
2 slug-abed sleepy-head
4 You take i.e. better take
4 pennyworths snatches (of sleep)
6 set . . . rest staked his all ("to venture one's final stake or reserve; from the old game of cards called primero, in which the loss of the "rest," i.e. the stakes kept in reserve . . . terminated the game"—OED)
7 God . . . me i.e. for that bawdy comment
10 take surprise (but with a sexual sense as well)
11 Will . . . be will nothing wake you
12 down back to bed
14ff Alas, alas our knowledge of Juliet's true condition assures comic detachment throughout this scene of vociferous mourning
15 weraday alas (III ii 38n)
16 aqua vitae spirits (III ii 90n)

LADY CAPULET. O me, O me! My child, my only life!
Revive, look up, or I will die with thee!
Help, help! Call help.

Enter Father.

FATHER. For shame, bring Juliet forth; her lord is come.

NURSE. She's dead, deceased; she's dead, alack the day! 25

MOTHER. Alack the day, she's dead, she's dead, she's dead!

CAPULET. Ha! let me see her. Out alas! she's cold,
Her blood is settled,° and her joints are stiff;
Life and these lips have long been separated.
Death lies on her like an untimely frost 30
Upon the sweetest flower of all the field.

NURSE. O lamentable day!

MOTHER. O woeful time!

CAPULET. Death, that hath ta'en her hence to make me wail,
Ties up my tongue and will not let me speak.° 35

Enter Friar [*Laurence*] *and the County* [*Paris, with Musicians*].

FRIAR. Come, is the bride ready to go to church?

CAPULET. Ready to go, but never to return.
O son, the night before thy wedding day
Hath Death lain with thy wife. There she lies,
Flower as she was, deflowerèd° by him. 40
Death is my son-in-law, Death is my heir;
My daughter he hath wedded. I will die
And leave him all. Life, living,° all is Death's.

PARIS. Have I thought° long to see this morning's face,
And doth it give me such a sight as this? 45
[*All at once cry out and wring their hands.*]°

MOTHER. Accursed, unhappy, wretched, hateful day!
Most miserable hour that e'er time saw
In lasting labor of his pilgrimage!°

---

28 settled returned to the heart, leaving Juliet pallid
35 will . . . speak it has been suggested that this is Shakespeare's little joke on Capulet, who is about to speak—abundantly
40 deflowerèd robbed of her virginity
43 living property
44 thought anticipated
45 s.d. from Q1 (their mourning at once both prevents the scene from dragging and renders it, for the audience, comic)
48 In . . . pilgrimage in his protracted toilsome course

But one, poor one, one poor and loving child,
But one thing to rejoice and solace in, 50
And cruel Death hath catched it from my sight.

NURSE. O woe! O woeful, woeful, woeful day!
Most lamentable day, most woeful day
That ever ever I did yet behold!
O day, O day, O day! O hateful day! 55
Never was seen so black a day as this.
O woeful day! O woeful day!

PARIS. Beguiled, divorcèd, wrongèd, spited, slain!
Most detestable° Death, by thee beguiled,
By cruel cruel thee quite overthrown. 60
O love! O life! not life, but love in death!

CAPULET. Despised, distressèd, hated, martyred, killed!
Uncomfortable° time, why cam'st thou now
To murder, murder our solemnity?°
O child, O child! my soul, and not my child! 65
Dead art thou—alack, my child is dead,
And with my child my joys are burièd!

FRIAR. Peace, ho, for shame! Confusion's cure lives not
In these confusions. Heaven and yourself
Had part in this fair maid—now heaven hath all, 70
And all the better is it for the maid.
Your part° in her you could not keep from death,
But heaven keeps his part° in eternal life.
The most you sought was her promotion,°
For 'twas your heaven she should be advanced; 75
And weep ye now, seeing she is advanced
Above the clouds, as high as heaven itself?
O, in this love,° you love your child so ill
That you run mad, seeing that she is well.°
She's not well married that lives married long, 80
But she's best married that dies married young.
Dry up your tears and stick your rosemary°

---

59 detestable pronounced détestáble
63 Uncomfortable comfortless
64 solemnity ceremony
72 Your part i.e. her body (which you begot)
73 his part i.e. her soul (which God gave)
74 promotion advancement in status (by marrying her to Paris)
78 in this love i.e. in this love which you are expressing in such boisterous grief
79 well well off (in heaven)
82 rosemary herb symbolizing remembrance

On this fair corse, and, as the custom is,
In all her best array bear her to church;
For though fond nature° bids us all lament, 85
Yet nature's tears are reason's merriment.°

CAPULET. All things that we ordainèd festival
Turn from their office° to black funeral—
Our instruments to melancholy bells,
Our wedding cheer to a sad burial feast; 90
Our solemn hymns to sullen dirges change;
Our bridal flowers serve for a buried corse;
And all things change them to the contrary.

FRIAR. Sir, go you in; and, madam, go with him;
And go, Sir Paris. Every one prepare 95
To follow this fair corse unto her grave.
The heavens do low'r° upon you for some ill;°
Move them no more by crossing their high will.

[*They all but the Nurse go forth, casting rosemary on her and shutting the curtains.*]°

[*Enter Musicians*]

1. MUSICIAN. Faith, we may put up our pipes and be gone.

NURSE. Honest good fellows, ah, put up, put up!° 100
For well you know this is a pitiful case.° [*Exit.*]°

1. MUSICIAN. Ay, by my troth, the case may be amended.°

Enter Peter.

PETER. Musicians, O, musicians, 'Heart's ease,'° 'Heart's ease'!
O, an you will have me live, play 'Heart's ease.'

1. MUSICIAN. Why 'Heart's ease'? 105

PETER. O, musicians, because my heart itself plays 'My heart

---

85 fond nature foolish human nature
86 reason's merriment what reason laughs at
88 office intended function
97 low'r frown
97 ill sin
98 s.d. from Q1; Q2 has *"Exeunt"*
100 put . . . up put away your instruments (but with an obvious sexual innuendo, carried on by the pun on *case*)
101 case (1) situation (2) instrument case (3) female sex organ
101 s.d. Q2 has *"Exit Omnes. Enter Will Kemp"*—Will Kemp being the name of the actor in Shakespeare's company who played Peter; the *Exit Omnes* may therefore mean that Shakespeare ended the scene here, but that later the company beefed up the role of Kemp, who was a popular comedian
102 amended (1) repaired (with reference to the instrument case) (2) improved (with reference to the Nurse, as in Mercutio's *old hare hoar:* see II iv 123 ff and notes)
103, 106-7 "Heart's ease," "My heart is full of woe" ballad tunes

is full of woe.' O, play me some merry dump° to comfort me.

1. MUSICIAN. Not a dump we! 'Tis no time to play now.

PETER. You will not then? 110

1. MUSICIAN. No.

PETER. I will then give it you soundly.

1. MUSICIAN. What will you give us?

PETER. No money, on my faith, but the gleek.° I will give you the minstrel.° 115

1. MUSICIAN. Then will I give you the serving-creature.°

PETER. Then will I lay the serving-creature's dagger on your pate. I will carry no crotchets.° I'll re you, I'll fa° you. Do you note me?°

1. MUSICIAN. An you re us and fa us, you note us.° 120

2. MUSICIAN. Pray you put up your dagger, and put out° your wit.

PETER. Then have at you with my wit! I will dry-beat° you with an iron wit,° and put up my iron dagger. Answer me like men. 125

'When griping grief the heart doth wound,
And doleful dumps° the mind oppress,
Then music with her silver sound'—
Why 'silver sound'? Why 'music with her silver sound'? What say you, Simon Catling?° 130

1. MUSICIAN. Marry, sir, because silver hath a sweet sound.

PETER. Pretty! What say you, Hugh Rebeck?°

2. MUSICIAN. I say 'silver sound' because musicians sound for silver.

PETER. Pretty too! What say you, James Soundpost?° 135

---

107 dump melancholy tune (on Shakespeare's part, but not Peter's, consciously incongruous with *merry)*
114 the gleek the mock
114-15 give . . . minstrel insultingly call you good for nothing
116 give . . . creature insultingly call you a menial
118 carry no crotchets put up with no whims (with pun on *crotchets* = quarter notes in musical notation)
118 re, fa names of musical notes
119 note me attend to me (with the obvious musical pun)
120 note us find fault with us (but again with the musical pun)
121 put out display
123 dry-beat thrash: see III i 77n
124 iron wit strong wit (with the implication, not intended by Peter, that it is also heavy)
127 doleful dumps melancholy moods
130 Catling lute string (made of cat-gut)
132 Rebeck three-stringed fiddle
135 Soundpost wooden peg supporting the bridge of a violin

3. MUSICIAN. Faith, I know not what to say.

PETER. O, I cry you mercy!° you are the singer. I will say for you. It is 'music with her silver sound' because musicians have no gold for sounding.°
'Then music with her silver sound 140
With speedy help doth lend redress.' *Exit.*

1. MUSICIAN. What a pestilent knave is this same!

2. MUSICIAN. Hang him, Jack!° Come, we'll in here, tarry for the mourners, and stay° dinner. *Exit [with others].*

Enter Romeo. V i

ROMEO. If I may trust the flattering° truth of sleep,
My dreams presage° some joyful news at hand.
My bosom's lord° sits lightly in his throne,
And all this day an unaccustomed spirit
Lifts me above the ground with cheerful thoughts. 5
I dreamt my lady came and found me dead
(Strange dream that gives a dead man leave to think!)
And breathed such life with kisses in my lips
That I revived and was an emperor.
Ah me! how sweet is love itself possessed, 10
When but love's shadows° are so rich in joy!

Enter Romeo's Man [Balthasar, booted°].

News from Verona! How now, Balthasar?
Dost thou not bring me letters from the friar?
How doth my lady? Is my father well?
How fares my Juliet? That I ask again, 15
For nothing can be ill if she be well.

---

137 Cry you mercy beg your pardon
139 sounding playing
143 Jack i.e. "the Jack" (= rude fellow)
144 stay wait for

V i 1 flattering (1) favorable (2) illusory
2 presage forecast
3 bosom's lord heart
11 shadows i.e. in dreams
11 s.d. Balthasar, booted from Q1
11 s.d. booted i.e. because he has just ridden from Verona

MAN. Then she is well, and nothing can be ill.
Her body sleeps in Capel's monument,°
And her immortal part with angels lives.
I saw her laid low in her kindred's vault 20
And presently° took post to tell it you.
O, pardon me for bringing these ill news,
Since you did leave it for my office,° sir.

ROMEO. Is it e'en so? Then I defy you, stars!°
Thou knowest my lodging. Get me ink and paper 25
And hire posthorses. I will hence to-night.

MAN. I do beseech you, sir, have patience.
Your looks are pale and wild and do import°
Some misadventure.

ROMEO. Tush,° thou art deceived. 30
Leave me and do the thing I bid thee do.
Hast thou no letters to me from the friar?

MAN. No, my good lord.

ROMEO. No matter. Get thee gone
And hire those horses. I'll be with thee straight. 35

Exit [*Balthasar*].

Well, Juliet, I will lie with thee to-night.
Let's see for means.° O mischief, thou art swift
To enter in the thoughts of desperate men!
I do remember an apothecary,
And hereabouts 'a dwells, which late I noted 40
In tatt'red weeds,° with overwhelming° brows,
Culling of simples.° Meagre were his looks,
Sharp misery had worn him to the bones;
And in his needy shop a tortoise hung,
An alligator stuffed, and other skins 45
Of ill-shaped fishes; and about his shelves
A beggarly account° of empty boxes,
Green earthen pots, bladders,° and musty seeds,

---

18 monument tomb
21 presently immediately
23 office duty
24 stars see Prologue to I i and I iv 113
28 import indicate, suggest
30 Tush "nonsense"
37 Let's . . . means how shall I go about it
41 weeds garments
41 overwhelming overhanging
42 Culling of simples collecting herbs
47 account number
48 bladders animal bladders prepared for use as floats

Remnants of packthread,° and old cakes of roses°
Where thinly scatterèd, to make up a show. 50
Noting this penury, to myself I said,
'An if a man did need a poison now
Whose sale is present° death in Mantua,
Here lives a caitiff° wretch would sell it him.'
O, this same thought did but forerun my need, 55
And this same needy man must sell it me.
As I remember, this should be the house.
Being holiday, the beggar's shop is shut.
What, ho! apothecary!

[*Enter Apothecary.*]

APOTHECARY. Who calls so loud? 60

ROMEO. Come hither, man. I see that thou art poor.
Hold, there is forty ducats.° Let me have
A dram° of poison, such soon-speeding gear°
As will disperse itself through all the veins
That the life-weary taker may fall dead, 65
And that the trunk° may be discharged of breath
As violently as hasty powder fired
Doth hurry from the fatal cannon's womb.

APOTHECARY. Such mortal° drugs I have; but Mantua's law
Is death to any he that utters° them. 70

ROMEO. Art thou so bare and full of wretchedness
And fearest to die? Famine is in thy cheeks,
Need and oppression starveth° in thy eyes,
Contempt and beggary hangs upon thy back:°
The world is not thy friend, nor the world's law; 75
The world affords no law to make thee rich;
Then be not poor, but break it and take this.

APOTHECARY. My poverty but not my will consents.

ROMEO. I pay thy poverty and not thy will.

---

49 packthread thread for tying packs
49 cakes of roses compressed rose petals (used as perfume)
53 present immediate
54 caitiff miserable
59 s.d. from Q1
62 ducat a gold coin
63 dram dose
63 soon . . . gear quick-killing stuff
66 trunk body
69 mortal deadly
70 utters gives out
73 starveth show their hunger
74 Contempt . . . back the contempt and beggary in which you live shows in your wretched clothing

APOTHECARY. Put this in any liquid thing you will 80
And drink it off, and if you had the strength
Of twenty men, it would dispatch you straight.

ROMEO. There is the gold—worse poison to men's souls,
Doing more murder in this loathsome world,
Than these poor compounds that thou mayst not sell. 85
I sell thee poison; thou hast sold me none.
Farewell. Buy food and get thyself in flesh.°
Come, cordial° and not poison, go with me
To Juliet's grave; for there must I use thee. *Exeunt.*

V ii

Enter Friar John to Friar Laurence.

JOHN. Holy Franciscan friar, brother, ho!

Enter [Friar] Laurence.

LAURENCE. This same should be the voice of Friar John.
Welcome from Mantua. What says Romeo?
Or, if his mind be writ, give me his letter.

JOHN. Going to find a barefoot brother out, 5
One of our order, to associate° me
Here in this city visiting the sick,
And finding him, the searchers° of the town,
Suspecting that we both were in a house
Where the infectious pestilence° did reign, 10
Sealed up the doors, and would not let us forth,
So that my speed to Mantua there was stayed.

LAURENCE. Who bare my letter, then, to Romeo?

JOHN. I could not send it—here it is again—
Nor get a messenger to bring it thee, 15
So fearful were they of infection.

---

87 in flesh fat
88 cordial literally, and here appropriately, a restorative for the heart
V ii 6 associate accompany
8 searchers health officers
10 pestilence plague

LAURENCE. Unhappy fortune! By my brotherhood,°
The letter was not nice,° but full of charge,°
Of dear import;° and the neglecting it
May do much danger. Friar John, go hence, 20
Get me an iron crow° and bring it straight
Unto my cell.

JOHN. Brother, I'll go and bring it thee. *Exit.*

LAURENCE. Now must I to the monument alone.
Within this three hours will fair Juliet wake. 25
She will beshrew° me much that Romeo
Hath had no notice of these accidents;°
But I will write again to Mantua,
And keep her at my cell till Romeo come—
Poor living corse, closed in a dead man's tomb! *Exit.* 30

Enter Paris and his Page [with flowers and sweet water°]. V iii

PARIS. Give me thy torch, boy. Hence, and stand aloof.
Yet put it out, for I would not be seen.
Under yond yew tree lay thee all along,°
Holding thy ear close to the hollow° ground.
So shall no foot upon the churchyard tread 5
(Being loose, unfirm, with digging up of graves)
But thou shalt hear it. Whistle then to me,
As signal that thou hearest something approach.
Give me those flowers. Do as I bid thee, go.

PAGE. [*aside*] I am almost afraid to stand alone 10
Here in the churchyard; yet I will adventure.° [*Retires.*]
[*Paris strews the tomb with flowers.*]°

---

17 my brotherhood i.e. my religious order
18 nice trivial
18 charge important business
19 dear import crucial importance
21 crow crowbar
26 beshrew reprove
27 accidents happenings
V iii s.d. with . . . water from Q1 (*sweet* = perfumed)
3 all along stretched out
4 hollow because so much excavated
11 adventure venture it
11 s.d. from Q1

PARIS. Sweet flower, with flowers thy bridal bed I strew
(O woe! thy canopy° is dust and stones)
Which with sweet water nightly I will dew;
Or, wanting that, with tears distilled by moans. 15
The obsequies° that I for thee will keep
Nightly shall be to strew thy grave and weep.

Whistle Boy.

The boy gives warning something doth approach.
What cursèd foot wanders this way to-night
To cross° my obsequies and true love's rite? 20
What, with a torch? Muffle° me, night, awhile. [*Retires.*]

Enter Romeo, [*and Balthasar with a torch, a mattock,*°
and a crow of iron°].

ROMEO. Give me that mattock and the wrenching iron.
Hold, take this letter. Early in the morning
See thou deliver it to my lord and father.
Give me the light. Upon thy life I charge thee, 25
Whate'er thou hearest or seest, stand all aloof
And do not interrupt me in my course.
Why I descend into this bed of death
Is partly to behold my lady's face,
But chiefly to take thence from her dead finger 30
A precious ring—a ring that I must use
In dear employment.° Therefore hence, be gone.
But if thou, jealous,° dost return to pry
In what I farther shall intend to do,
By heaven, I will tear thee joint by joint 35
And strew this hungry° churchyard with thy limbs.
The time and my intents are savage-wild,
More fierce and more inexorable far
Than empty° tigers or the roaring sea.

BALTHASAR. I will be gone, sir, and not trouble you. 40

---

13 canopy bed canopy
16 obsequies commemorative funeral rites
20 cross frustrate
21 Muffle i.e. hide
21 s.d. and Balthasar . . . iron from Q1; Q2 has *Enter Romeo and Peter*—either because that is the name of Romeo's man in the source poem and Shakespeare momentarily forgot he had already given him the name of Balthasar, or, more probably, because the actor who played Balthasar doubled as Peter
21 s.d. mattock pick axe **crow** crowbar
32 dear employment important business
33 jealous suspicious
36 hungry i.e. because thought of as a devourer
39 empty unfed

ROMEO. So shalt thou show me friendship. Take thou that.°
Live, and be prosperous; and farewell, good fellow.

BALTHASAR. [*aside*] For all this same, I'll hide me hereabout.
His looks I fear,° and his intents I doubt.° [*Retires.*]

ROMEO. Thou detestable° maw,° thou womb of death, 45
Gorged with the dearest morsel of the earth,
Thus I enforce thy rotten jaws to open,
And in despite I'll cram thee with more food.°
[*Romeo opens the tomb.*]°

PARIS. This is that banished haughty Montague
That murd'red my love's cousin—with which grief 50
It is supposèd the fair creature died—
And here is come to do some villainous shame
To the dead bodies. I will apprehend° him.
Stop thy unhallowèd toil, vile Montague!
Can vengeance° be pursued further than death? 55
Condemnèd villain, I do apprehend thee.
Obey, and go with me; for thou must die.

ROMEO. I must indeed; and therefore came I hither.
Good gentle youth, tempt not a desp'rate man.
Fly hence and leave me. Think upon these gone;° 60
Let them affright thee. I beseech thee, youth,
Put not another sin upon my head
By urging me to fury. O, be gone!
By heaven, I love thee better than myself,
For I come hither armed against myself. 65
Stay not, be gone. Live, and hereafter say
A madman's mercy bid thee run away.

PARIS. I do defy thy conjuration°
And apprehend thee for a felon here.

ROMEO. Wilt thou provoke me? Then have at thee, boy! 70
[*They fight.*]

---

41 that i.e. money
44 I fear am made apprehensive by
44 doubt am suspicious of
45 detestable pronounced détestáble
45 maw stomach
48 in . . . food to spite you (for devouring Juliet) I'll force more food into you (i.e. my own body) though you are already gorged
48 s.d. from Q1
53 apprehend arrest
55 vengeance i.e. on Tybalt
60 gone dead (i.e. as a warning of what you too will be if you do not fly at once)
68 conjuration warning

PAGE. O Lord, they fight! I will go call the watch.°
[*Exit. Paris falls.*]

PARIS. O, I am slain! If thou be merciful,
Open the tomb, lay me with Juliet. [*Dies.*]

ROMEO. In faith, I will. Let me peruse this face.
Mercutio's kinsman, noble County Paris! 75
What said my man when my betossèd soul
Did not attend° him as we rode? I think
He told me Paris should have married Juliet.
Said he not so? or did I dream it so?
Or am I mad, hearing him talk of Juliet, 80
To think it was so? O, give me thy hand,
One writ with me in sour misfortune's book!
I'll bury thee in a triumphant grave.
A grave? O, no, a lanthorn,° slaught'red youth,
For here lies Juliet, and her beauty makes 85
This vault a feasting presence° full of light.
Death, lie thou there, by a dead man interred.
[*Lays him in the tomb.*]
How oft when men are at the point of death
Have they been merry! which their keepers° call
A lightning° before death. O, how may I 90
Call this a lightning? O my love! my wife!
Death, that hath sucked the honey of thy breath,
Hath had no power yet upon the beauty.
Thou art not conquered. Beauty's ensign° yet
Is crimson in thy lips and in thy cheeks, 95
And death's pale flag is not advancèd there.
Tybalt, liest thou there in thy bloody sheet?
O, what more favor can I do to thee
Than with that hand that cut thy youth in twain
To sunder his° that was thine enemy? 100
Forgive me, cousin! Ah, dear Juliet,
Why art thou yet so fair?° Shall I believe
That unsubstantial Death is amorous,

---

71 watch nightwatchman
77 attend pay attention to
84 lanthorn windowed turret, i.e. a bright open place
86 presence room of state where royalty is accustomed to be "present" to receive official guests
89 keepers jailers
90 lightning lightening (of spirits) but with pun on *lightening* = a lighting up
94 ensign flag
100 his i.e. his youth (= life)
102 Why . . . fair her color is presumably restored as she nears the time of waking

And that the lean abhorrèd monster keeps
Thee here in dark to be his paramour? 105
For fear of that I still will stay with thee
And never from this palace of dim night
Depart again. Here, here will I remain
With worms that are thy chambermaids. O, here
Will I set up my everlasting rest° 110
And shake the yoke of inauspicious stars
From this world-wearied flesh. Eyes, look your last!
Arms, take your last embrace! and, lips, O you
The doors of breath, seal with a righteous kiss
A dateless° bargain to engrossing° death! 115
Come, bitter conduct;° come, unsavory guide!
Thou desperate pilot, now at once run on
The dashing rocks thy seasick weary bark!°
Here's to my love! [*Drinks.*] O true apothecary!
Thy drugs are quick.° Thus with a kiss I die. [*Falls.*]° 120

Enter Friar [*Laurence*], *with lanthorn,° crow, and spade.*

FRIAR. Saint Francis be my speed!° how oft to-night
Have my old feet stumbled° at graves! Who's there?

BALTHASAR. Here's one, a friend, and one that knows you well.

FRIAR. Bliss be upon you! Tell me, good my friend,
What torch is yond that vainly lends his light 125
To grubs and eyeless skulls? As I discern,
It burneth in the Capels' monument.

BALTHASAR. It doth so, holy sir; and there's my master.
One that you love.

FRIAR. Who is it? 130

BALTHASAR. Romeo.

FRIAR. How long hath he been there?

BALTHASAR. Full half an hour.

FRIAR. Go with me to the vault.

---

110 set . . . rest stake all (see IV v 6)
115 dateless timeless
115 engrossing all encompassing (but with a pun on *engross* = to corner the market in a commodity)
116 conduct guide (with a glance forward to *pilot*, 117)
118 bark ship (see II ii 85-87)
120 quick (1) speedy (in operation) (2) life-giving (in reuniting me with Juliet)
120 s.d. from Q1; **lanthorn** lantern
121 speed help
122 stumbled (a bad omen)

BALTHASAR. I dare not, sir. 135
My master knows not but I am gone hence,
And fearfully did menace me with death
If I did stay to look on his intents.

FRIAR. Stay then; I'll go alone. Fear comes upon me.
O, much I fear some ill unthrifty° thing. 140

BALTHASAR. As I did sleep under this yew tree here,
I dreamt my master and another fought,
And that my master slew him.

FRIAR. Romeo!
[Friar stoops and looks on the blood and weapons.]°
Alack, alack, what blood is this which stains 145
The stony entrance of this sepulchre?
What mean these masterless and gory swords
To lie discolored by this place of peace? *[Enters the tomb.]*
Romeo! O, pale! Who else? What, Paris too?
And steeped in blood? Ah, what an unkind° hour 150
Is guilty of this lamentable chance!
The lady stirs. *[Juliet rises.]*

JULIET. O comfortable° friar! where is my lord?
I do remember well where I should be,
And there I am. Where is my Romeo? 155

FRIAR. I hear some noise. Lady, come from that nest
Of death, contagion, and unnatural sleep.
A greater power than we can contradict
Hath thwarted our intents. Come, come away.
Thy husband in thy bosom there lies dead; 160
And Paris too. Come, I'll dispose of thee
Among a sisterhood of holy nuns.
Stay not to question, for the watch is coming.
Come, go, good Juliet. I dare no longer stay.

JULIET. Go, get thee hence, for I will not away. *Exit [Friar].* 165
What's here? A cup, closed in my true love's hand?
Poison, I see, hath been his timeless° end.
O churl!° drunk all, and left no friendly drop

---

140 unthrifty unfortunate
144 s.d. from Q1
150 unkind unnatural
153 comfortable comforting
167 timeless untimely
168 churl rude fellow (the tone and spirit of Juliet's "O churl!" is affectionate and playful, i.e. "What, no manners?")

To help me after? I will kiss thy lips.
Haply some poison yet doth hang on them 170
To make me die with a restorative. [*Kisses him.*]
Thy lips are warm!

CHIEF WATCHMAN. [*within*] Lead, boy. Which way?

JULIET. Yea, noise? Then I'll be brief. O happy° dagger!
[*Snatches Romeo's dagger.*]
This is thy sheath; there rust,° and let me die. 175
[*She stabs herself and falls.*]°

Enter [*Paris's*] *Boy and Watch.*

BOY. This is the place. There, where the torch doth burn.

CHIEF WATCHMAN. The ground is bloody. Search about the churchyard.
Go, some of you; whoe'er you find attach.
[*Exeunt some of the Watch.*]
Pitiful sight! here lies the County slain;
And Juliet bleeding, warm, and newly dead, 180
Who here hath lain this two days burièd.
Go, tell the Prince; run to the Capulets;
Raise up the Montagues; some others search.
[*Exeunt others of the Watch.*]
We see the ground whereon these woes do lie,
But the true ground° of all these piteous woes 185
We cannot without circumstance° descry.

Enter [*some of the Watch, with*] *Romeo's Man* [*Balthasar*].

2. WATCHMAN. Here's Romeo's man. We found him in the churchyard.

CHIEF WATCHMAN. Hold him in safety till the Prince comes hither.

Enter Friar [*Laurence*] *and another Watchman.*

3. WATCHMAN. Here is a friar that trembles, sighs, and weeps.
We took this mattock and this spade from him 190
As he was coming from this churchyard side.

---

174 happy opportune—but with a pun (for the audience) on *happy* = lucky, blissful
175 rust remain forever (wasting away as all things temporal must, yet a lasting witness to my fidelity to Romeo); many editors adopt Q1's *rest* as being less grotesque or preposterous, but the grotesqueness may be part of Juliet's defiant giving of herself to Romeo's dagger, and therefore part of Shakespeare's intention
175 s.d. from Q1
185 ground basis
186 circumstance details

CHIEF WATCHMAN. A great suspicion! Stay the friar too.

Enter the Prince [*and Attendants*°].

PRINCE. What misadventure is so early up,
That calls our person from our morning rest?

Enter Capulet and his Wife° [*with others*].

CAPULET. What should it be, that is so shrieked abroad? 195

WIFE. The people in the street cry 'Romeo,'
Some 'Juliet,' and some 'Paris'; and all run,
With open outcry, toward our monument.

PRINCE. What fear is this which startles in your ears?

CHIEF WATCHMAN. Sovereign, here lies the County Paris slain; 200
And Romeo dead; and Juliet, dead before,
Warm and new killed.

PRINCE. Search, seek, and know how this foul murder comes.

CHIEF WATCHMAN. Here is a friar, and slaughtered Romeo's man,
With instruments upon them fit to open 205
These dead men's tombs.

CAPULET. O heavens! O wife, look how our daughter bleeds!
This dagger hath mista'en, for, lo, his house°
Is empty on the back of Montague,
And it missheathèd in my daughter's bosom! 210

WIFE. O me! this sight of death is as a bell°
That warns my old age° to a sepulcher.

Enter Montague [*and others*].

PRINCE. Come, Montague; for thou art early up
To see thy son and heir more early down.

MONTAGUE. Alas, my liege, my wife is dead to-night! 215
Grief of my son's exile hath stopped her breath.
What further woe conspires against mine age?

---

192 s.d. and Attendants Q1 has *with others*
194 s.d. Enter . . . Wife from Q1; Q2 has *Enter Capels*
208 his house its sheath
211 bell i.e. the bell that was formerly tolled to signalize a death (to which Donne's famous sentence alludes: "Never send to know for whom the bell tolls: it tolls for thee")
212 my old age i.e. she has been through so much that she feels old and ready to die (at the play's opening Shakespeare seems to conceive of her as aged 28, but age in his plays generally is an emotional not a chronological matter)

PRINCE. Look, and thou shalt see.

MONTAGUE. O thou untaught!° what manners is in this,
To press before thy father to a grave? 220

PRINCE. Seal up the mouth of outrage° for a while,
Till we can clear these ambiguities
And know their spring, their head, their true descent;
And then will I be general of your woes°
And lead you even to death.° Meantime forbear, 225
And let mischance be slave to patience.°
Bring forth the parties of suspicion.

FRIAR. I am the greatest,° able to do least,°
Yet most suspected, as the time and place
Doth make against me, of this direful murder; 230
And here I stand, both to impeach and purge°
Myself condemnèd and myself excused.

PRINCE. Then say at once what thou dost know in this.

FRIAR. I will be brief, for my short date of breath°
Is not so long as is a tedious tale. 235
Romeo, there dead, was husband to that Juliet;
And she, there dead, that Romeo's faithful wife.
I married them; and their stol'n marriage day
Was Tybalt's doomsday, whose untimely death
Banished the new-made bridegroom from this city; 240
For whom, and not for Tybalt, Juliet pined.
You, to remove that siege of grief from her,
Betrothed and would have married her perforce°
To County Paris. Then comes she to me
And with wild looks bid me devise some mean 245
To rid her from this second marriage,
Or in my cell there would she kill herself.
Then gave I her (so tutored by my art)

---

219 untaught i.e. untaught a proper respect for your elders
221 outrage angry outcry
224 general . . . woes leader of your grieving
225 even to death (1) even if grief kills us? (2) even to application of the death penalty (when the truth is all known)?
226 let . . . patience let the passions roused by these misfortunes submit to patience
228 greatest i.e. greatest suspicion
228 least because an old man and a friar
231 impeach and purge accuse myself where I deserve it, exonerate myself where I deserve it
234 short . . . of breath life expectancy (like Lady Capulet, the Friar lives in emotional not chronological time)
243 perforce by force

A sleeping potion; which so took effect
As I intended, for it wrought on her 250
The form of death. Meantime I writ to Romeo
That he should hither come as° this dire night
To help to take her from her borrowèd grave,
Being the time the potion's force should cease.
But he which bore my letter, Friar John, 255
Was stayed by accident, and yesternight
Returned my letter back. Then all alone
At the prefixèd hour of her waking
Came I to take her from her kindred's vault;
Meaning to keep her closely° at my cell 260
Till I conveniently could send to Romeo.
But when I came, some minute ere the time
Of her awakening, here untimely lay
The noble Paris and true Romeo dead.
She wakes; and I entreated her come forth 265
And bear this work of heaven with patience;
But then a noise did scare me from the tomb,
And she, too desperate, would not go with me,
But, as it seems, did violence on herself.
All this I know, and to the marriage 270
Her nurse is privy;° and if aught in this
Miscarried by my fault, let my old life
Be sacrificed, some hour before his time,
Unto the rigor of severest law.

PRINCE. We still° have known thee for a holy man. 275
Where's Romeo's man? What can he say to this?

BALTHASAR. I brought my master news of Juliet's death;
And then in post he came from Mantua
To this same place, to this same monument.
This letter he early° bid me give his father, 280
And threat'ned me with death, going in the vault,
If I departed not and left him there.

PRINCE. Give me the letter. I will look on it.
Where is the County's page that raised the watch?
Sirrah, what made° your master in this place? 285

---

252 as on
260 closely hidden
270-71 to . . . privy of . . . informed
275 still always
280 early modifies *give*
285 made did

BOY. He came with flowers to strew his lady's grave;
And bid me stand aloof, and so I did.
Anon° comes one with light to ope the tomb;
And by and by° my master drew on him;
And then I ran away to call the watch. 290

PRINCE. This letter doth make good the friar's words,
Their course of love, the tidings of her death;
And here he writes that he did buy a poison
Of a poor pothecary, and therewithal°
Came to this vault to die, and lie with Juliet. 295
Where be these enemies? Capulet, Montague,
See what a scourge is laid upon your hate,
That heaven finds means to kill your joys with love.
And I, winking at° your discords too,
Have lost a brace° of kinsmen. All are punished. 300

CAPULET. O brother Montague, give me thy hand.
This° is my daughter's jointure,° for no more
Can I demand.

MONTAGUE. But I can give thee more;
For I will raise her statue in pure gold, 305
That whiles Verona by that name is known,
There shall no figure at such rate° be set
As that of true and faithful Juliet.

CAPULET. As rich shall Romeo's° by his lady's lie—
Poor sacrifices° of our enmity! 310

PRINCE. A glooming° peace this morning with it brings.
The sun for sorrow will not show his head.
Go hence, to have more talk of these sad things;
Some shall be pardoned, and some punishèd;
For never was a story of more woe 315
Than this of Juliet and her Romeo. [*Exeunt omnes.*]

---

288 Anon soon
289 by and by immediately
294 therewithal therewith
299 winking at closing my eyes to
300 brace pair (Mercutio and Paris)
302 This the handshake indicating their reconciliation
302 jointure the estate reserved for the wife, to be her support after her husband's death
307 rate value
309 Romeo's i.e. a golden effigy of Romeo
310 Poor sacrifices i.e. the statues are a poor atonement for the enmity that has lost us our children
311 glooming (1) overcast (2) troubled

STUDY QUESTIONS

ESSAY QUESTIONS

1. Take as your lead any of the following comments on *Romeo and Juliet* and write a paper developing the idea, or qualifying it, or refuting it—or a combination of all three:
(a) "That *Romeo and Juliet* is a tragedy of fate can hardly be doubted. Shakespeare says as much in the Prologue. The lovers are marked for death; their fortunes are 'crossed' by the stars. . . . The numerous mischances experienced by the lovers are not fortuitous bad luck but represent the working out of some hidden design. Critics who attack the play for lacking inevitability have misunderstood Shakespeare's dramatic technique. Like Hamlet's adventures with the pirates, the sequence of mishaps here is deliberately made so improbable that chance alone cannot explain it. Only fate, or the will of Heaven, affords a sufficient explanation."
(b) "On the surface, social evil is castigated and purged by 'Fate,' which is an extra-human moral order. Yet in contrast to this often declared thesis, and by no means reconciled with it, Shakespeare intrudes a line of thinking which was to become central in his serious philosophy: that the cause of tragedy lies in the sufferers themselves. . . . The dangerous fault of the two lovers is their extreme rashness."
(c) "To convey his vivid intuition of the place and duration of love in the dark world of time, Shakespeare finds the lightning-in-the-night adequate as the germinating and organizing symbol for *Romeo and Juliet*. . . . Yet since the dark shades of hate are here little more than the touches of an artist designed to set off the brilliant lightning flashes of passion, *Romeo and Juliet* shows less the tragedy than the pathos of pure love: 'So quick bright things come to confusion! [ruin]' [*A Midsummer Night's Dream,* I i 151]."
(d) "The sense of triumph descends upon the play from a love so straight, so simple, and so certain that its very bravery transforms death and time and hatred—yes, and the accidents of Fate—into insubstantial shadows. The quick bright things remain shining and alive."

(e) "... [Mercutio] exists more as a character portrayed for its own innate interest than as an essential participant in the dramatic action."
(f) "... Juliet's 'ancient damnation' is [a] succinct description of [the Nurse's] sin. What more ancient damnation is there than sensuality—and all the other sins it brings in its train? Those who dismiss the Nurse as just a coarse old woman whose loquacity makes us laugh fail hopelessly to plumb the depths of her depravity."
(g) "... there is just one agency powerful enough in youth to defy and cut across [the] domination of the generations, and that is love.... Hostility simply has nothing to breathe in such a transcendental atmosphere. It is through the effect of their love on both lovers, and the poetry in which they spontaneously embody it, that Shakespeare convinces us it is no mere infatuation, but love indeed in its divine sense. Passion it is, of course, but that contaminated term has in our day become helpless to express it. Purity would be the perfect word for it if the world had not forgotten that purity is simply Greek for fire."
(h) "If *Romeo and Juliet* celebrates the beauty and grace of young love, it is also, in its language, Shakespeare's dirtiest play. The grossness of the Nurse is essential for understanding the luminous innocence of Juliet, and Mercutio's witty pornography sets off the intensity of Romeo's commitment."

STUDY QUESTIONS

[*I i*]

1. Characterize Sampson and Gregory and the quality of their verbal exchange: is it funny or just crude? belligerent or a way to pump up their courage? What is there to be scared of?
2. What do you think Sampson and Gregory should look like? Do they differ in personality and in other qualities? How would you bring these differences out in casting actors to play the parts? in directing their manner of speaking? To what extent do you think they should both look different from Abram and his companion?
3. From how many pieces of evidence in the first scene, in addition to the servants' behavior, may we argue that one of the two families is more "feud-minded" than the other? Do not overlook the evidence in the Prince's declamation (77–99), or the subtler evidence in the discourse of Benvolio, Lady Montague, and Montague right after the brawl (100–56).

4. What is the point of bringing Romeo in when the brawl is *ended*? Why not involve him in it at once? What is his attitude toward it? What feelings does he have that produce that attitude?
5. What clues are given in Romeo's speeches to Benvolio suggest that he is more interested in "being in love" than in the girl?
6. How many reasons can you think of for beginning a play about love with a conflict?

[*I ii*]

1. How is the action in Scene ii tied to what has happened in Scene i? In what specific ways is the plot advanced? What innocent decisions made here—and what coincidences—support the comment in the Prologue that the lovers are "star-crossed"?
2. How does Romeo's language in lines 91–96 prepare for the language he uses when he first sees and then talks to Juliet (I v 45–54, 97–114)? How is the later language different in tone?

[*I iii*]

1. Scene iii brings the female world of the play into focus. What necessary information is introduced?
2. What sort of people do you take Lady Capulet and the Nurse to be? Describe the impressions you would want the actresses playing each role to communicate to the audience. What things do we learn about the Nurse from her long story of Juliet's infancy? and what about Lady Capulet from her long comparison of love to a book? What has happened to old Capulet's demurrers about his daughter's ripeness for marriage?
3. Juliet says practically nothing while the Nurse prattles on and her mother tries to get her message in edgewise. What do her words suggest to you: docile obedience? indifference to talkative old women? self-control? the wisdom to know when to keep one's own counsel? If you were directing the play or playing the part, what would you have Juliet do during this scene? What attitudes would you want the audience to have towards Juliet?

[*I iv*]

1. It takes a careful reading of the notes to follow all the banter in this scene. How is this punning and needling different from that between the servants in Scene i and what does it indicate about the difference between the two groups of peo-

ple? Are the Maskers looking for trouble? (Not all have been invited, but Mercutio and perhaps some others have been.) Why do they want to crash the party? What two moods are contrasted in Romeo and Mercutio?

2. What brings Queen Mab to Mercutio's mind? What is his aim in discoursing on her to Romeo—what is he seeking to discredit? What does the speech add to our impressions of Mercutio in earlier parts of the scene?
3. What do you make of Romeo's words in lines 112–19? Do they grow out of anything we have seen in him thus far? Are they simply another expression of his love-sickness, his self-absorption, or are they something different altogether?

[*I v*]

1. The telescoping of time that occurs throughout Act I is probably more disturbing to a reader (especially one who wrongly expects play action to have some reasonable relationship to what he knows of time in the real world) than to a theatergoer. Putting yourself in the director's role, suggest how you would handle this scene to indicate that all is not so rapidly concluded as the briefness in print seems to show, even though one of the hallmarks of this play is a precipitate rush to a conclusion.
2. What kind of person is old Capulet shown to be in this scene? Support your judgment with details of what he says and does. To what extent do his comments about Romeo give us a new and different angle on that young man? What do you take to be the point of the episode (29–41) where the two elderly Capulets comment on the passage of time?
3. What about Capulet himself? Is he a Tybalt grown old? Why or why not? How would you characterize Tybalt's behavior in this scene? If you were playing the part, do you see any grounds for suggesting that he is other than a surly brawler? Explain.
4. What in Scenes i and ii have prepared us not to be surprised by Romeo's fervent outburst of admiration for Juliet? In that outburst, what does he recognize about his past feelings? How does the language he now uses differ from his talk about Rosaline?

[*II i*]

1. The party's over, the guests have gone, and Romeo once again gives his friends the slip, but for a different reason this time, as he says in lines 1–2. His words at the opening of II ii tell us

that he hears everything that Mercutio and Benvolio say. Is that Mercutio's intention? Do you think Mercutio assumes that Romeo hears him? How do you know? Imagine that you are directing the play: what advice would you give to Romeo and Mercutio about how to handle their parts to give the audience the impression you think they should get of Mercutio declaiming and Romeo listening?

2. Mercutio talks with deliberate vulgarity. How do his words, meant for Romeo's ears, help us recognize that the new attachment to Juliet is a far different thing from Romeo's mooning over Rosaline? Would Mercutio change his tune if he knew that Juliet had supplanted Rosaline? Why or why not? What is "love" to Mercutio, no matter who is involved?

[*II ii*]

1. What contrasts do you see between this scene and the preceding one in what is talked about and in the language used? How is the quality of the love-making here thoroughly different from that which Mercutio harps on? What hints do we get in all this joyful talk that the course of true love is not going to run smooth?
2. What samenesses and differences do you see in how Romeo and Juliet reveal themselves in the language they use? Consider especially, for Romeo, lines 12–16, 22–25, 27–33, 69–72, 85–87, 110–11, 144–46, 163–65, 198–99; for Juliet, lines 34–37, 54–55, 65–68, 95–104, 112–14, 133–34, 147–53, 187–92.
3. One critic has said, in commenting on the confrontation in this scene, that it reveals "the mutual sense of awe and fear" the two young lovers have in this unplanned meeting soon after the brief encounter at old Capulet's party. Show that the observation is accurate or inaccurate, or maybe a little of both.
4. Characterize, or define, "love" as it is revealed in this scene. How convinced are you that these two are not just playing essentially the same game that Romeo was playing before?

[*II iii*]

1. What do you see as the purpose of the Friar's opening soliloquy? What does he say (and believe) that Nature can do, with a knowing assist from humans? What further meaning is added after Romeo's entrance? In the light of what happens, would you say that the Friar heeds his own advice? Explain. If you were directing the play, would you have the Friar give the audience a hint that he is aware of Romeo's entrance

even though he doesn't let Romeo know? Why or why not?

2. How seriously does the Friar take the switch of Romeo's love to Juliet? Why has Romeo gone to him in the first place? Why does the Friar even consider marrying Romeo and Juliet? What is his attitude toward "love" and the two lovers?
3. Much of the effect of this scene, when acted, comes from the vivid contrast between age (and its deliberateness) and youth (and its impetuousness). How often have we seen this contrast before?

[*II iv*]

1. What does Mercutio's extended outburst about Tybalt and the kind of behavior he affects prepare us for in the later street scene? What in Mercutio's view makes Romeo not "a man to encounter Tybalt"? What exactly does he deplore about Tybalt's behavior? Could it be argued that he deplores in Romeo what he believes to be another version of the same thing? Consider lines 82–86 (i.e., "Now art . . . nature").
2. It takes some wit (and some work for modern readers) to follow the verbal thrusts and parries of Romeo and Mercutio. Up to now, we've had only brief suggestions that Romeo could match Mercutio in witty rejoinders, yet here he beats him. Coming on the heels of the transcendent seriousness of his meetings with Juliet and the Friar, does this coarse joking throw doubt on the honesty of Romeo's protestations and preparations or does it emphasize their honesty by the contrast between his present exuberance and his former moping?
3. Mercutio shifts targets when the Nurse appears. How is she dressed? What is she affecting to be? Is she still a third version of a fault that Shakespeare has already satirized in Romeo (II i) and Tybalt (II iii)? If you were playing the part, or directing someone playing it, how would you act out the Nurse's responses to the ribald attention she gets from Mercutio? Can it be said that she asks for what she gets? What part is she trying to play? What part does she end up playing?
4. Characterize Romeo as you see him in both parts of this scene. What sides of him are revealed that haven't been shown before?

[*II v*]

1. This scene unfolds another of the marvelously contrasting moods of the play. What sides of Juliet are revealed that we haven't seen before? Shakespeare means her to be quite

young and innocent, but he certainly doesn't mean her to be simply a child. How does her behavior here help to establish that distinction? Notice that most of the language of the scene is blunt and natural, quite unlike that of the earlier scene between her and Romeo, where the stylized verbal love-play sets a totally different mood.

2. Why do you suppose the Nurse gives Juliet such a hard time? Does she seek to moderate the effect of the good news on Juliet or to intensify it?
3. In what respect is the contrast of moods here similar to that in II iii?
4. This is an excellent short scene to use for carefully prepared readings, with several pairs of readers taking turns. Try to decide what you want to show about the kind of relationship these two people have, determine how certain key lines should be handled (for instance, for Juliet lines 27–28, 31–37, 54, 58–61, 66; for the Nurse 29–30, 38–45, 55–57, 62–65), and then do some rehearsing together. After the pairs have presented their interpretations, have the audience discuss their faithfulness to the language of the scene.

[*II vi*]

1. How do the Friar's brief opening words (1–2) and Romeo's response (3–8) immediately create a striking and sobering contrast to the two preceding scenes? The import of their comments is ominous for the audience, but do you suppose that either man sees them that way? They both know the dangers that the coming marriage is surrounded by, but is that what is principally on their minds in speaking as they speak; in other words, is what they say perfectly consonant with Romeo's feelings of joy and the Friar's recognition of his proper moralizing role even if there were no known danger connected with the marriage? If so, why are these lines ironic as well as prophetic, and not in the least heavy-handed or gloomy?
2. What do you make of the brief and reserved greetings of Romeo and Juliet and their following comments? They can speak plainly enough about their passion for each other; what is their language meant to convey here?
3. What powerful effects would be lost if this brief scene were omitted in production? Consider the nature of the two scenes that precede it and the one that follows.

[*III i*]

1. What is the purpose of Mercutio's humorous needling of Benvolio about his quarrelsomeness? What is ironic about it? What do you make of Mercutio so far? He's witty, and he has shown an ability to penetrate through posturings and poses of all kinds. What other qualities would you attribute to him, taking all of this scene into account? One student said of him: "With friends like Mercutio, who needs enemies?" Do you agree with that? Why or why not?
2. Why is Tybalt out looking for Romeo? He talks of the "injuries" Romeo has done him. What injuries? Why doesn't Tybalt respond hotly to Mercutio's taunting if he's simply looking for a fight? Why does Romeo's conciliatory treatment of Tybalt anger Mercutio? One critic has characterized this scene as being built around the "interaction of ill-doing and ill-luck." Which participants may be credited with some "ill-doing"? which with "ill-luck"?
3. Twice Mercutio says, "A plague a both your houses!" In the light of the entire play, this may seem a fitting comment for anyone to make, but how appropriate is it coming from Mercutio here?
4. Why does Romeo decide to confront Tybalt? To avenge Mercutio's death? Any other reason(s)? Describe the Romeo of lines 108–14, 118–19, and 121–28. Is his decision one of "ill-doing" or of "ill-luck," as the phrases are used in Question 2? He says in line 136, "O, I am fortune's fool!" Is he?
5. Why do you suppose the playwright brings the Prince, the Montagues, the Capulets, "and all" on stage quickly following the "Citizens"? How does their behavior echo the brawling behavior we have just witnessed? What is the purpose of Benvolio's long explanation of what has happened? How accurate is it? What does the Prince's final comment in the scene echo from a previous scene about a brawl?

[*III ii*]

1. Many producers of the play eliminate most of Juliet's speech at the beginning of this scene, probably because they feel that most audiences won't be able to cope with it. Perhaps modern audiences can't square such high-flown rhetoric with such a young girl, but if so, there's a lot of the play that will go unappreciated, as we have seen. What is lost by cutting these lines (1–31)? Consider what they suggest about her frame of mind, the intensity of her expectations, the depth of her feelings for Romeo, physical and otherwise. What are we meant to see in her that goes well beyond her years?

2. How is the Nurse's failure to get to the point a totally different thing here from the teasing she indulged herself in earlier (II v)? What is the reason for it here? How genuine is her woe-crying? What conflicting emotions are tearing Juliet apart that the Nurse clearly neither understands nor could understand? How do the intricate puns of lines 45–53 and the multiple paradoxes of lines 75–87 underscore the intensity of Juliet's confusion and her recognition of ruined joys and expectations? What keeps all this wild and sustained lamenting from being silly or ludicrous? Are we meant to see parts of the scene as comical? If so, which parts?
3. The Nurse turns off her woe rather suddenly in lines 88–92 with a simple-minded listing of the failings of men in general, a call for a drink to soothe her "griefs," and a not very strongly worded condemnation of Romeo. Why does Juliet react so fiercely? What does her answer to the Nurse's "Will you speak well of him that killed your cousin?" show both about the agony of the choice she must make and the steadfastness she will show in making that choice? Specifically, what does she commit herself to in lines 100–40?
4. What does it tell us about the Nurse that she offers to summon Romeo and to see to it that Romeo's wedding-night visit will be as originally planned? Why does she do so? How does her behavior in III v shed light on her behavior here?

[*III iii*]

1. What does it tell us about both Romeo and Juliet that they find banishment worse than death? To the practical mind, banishment lays open possibilities of a reconciliation elsewhere or a change of mind on the part of the banisher. But these two find the separation of the moment the only reality that means anything. What do you make of Romeo's argument (line 30–52) supporting his contention that "banishèd is death mistermed"?
2. What advice does the Friar offer, both before and after the Nurse arrives? Why does Romeo scorn it initially? How would you have him react during the Friar's harangue (113–63)? Does he accept what's being said, or doesn't it matter now that he's about to go to Juliet? In what ways is the Friar sensible but also foolish?
3. What is comical in this scene? How would you compare and contrast its effects with those in II ii, II iv, II v, III ii?

[*III iv*]

1. What do you see as the purpose of this scene? Capulet has

previously said that he was in no hurry to have Juliet marry, yet now he's in a haste to marry her to Paris despite the mourning for Tybalt. (Tybalt's death, in fact, is used as the excuse for the haste, here and in III v.) If there seems to be no reasonable explanation of this change of mind on Capulet's part, what is the dramatic justification on the playwright's part? How does this turn of events confront Romeo and Juliet with dwindling options?

[*III v*]

1. The love-talk here between Romeo and Juliet is of a kind with that of their earlier scenes together, but it is in a decidedly lower key. How do you account for that?
2. What hints are there of desperation here, either in what is said or suggested? What hints are there that the two of them may be seeing the banishment as the Frair sees it and not as the end of things? What's the dramatic value of giving the first part of this scene a "hushed and plaintive quality," as one critic puts it, coming as it does after Capulet's promise to Paris and before his and his wife's explosion at Juliet's refusal to accept Paris?
3. The exchange between Juliet and her mother is a masterpiece of verbal dueling on Juliet's part. What does it show about her position that she has to play such games? How does her mother's revelation about Paris change her behavior? Why can't she equivocate about that too?
4. Old Capulet brutally demolishes Juliet's brave show to her mother and to him. The starch momentarily gone, she can only ask for sympathy and understanding. What does she get in return from her father, her mother, and, finally, the Nurse (who had for a moment stood up to the old man's anger)? What options do these successive jolts leave her?

[*IV i*]

1. Paris is an unwitting accomplice in the disaster that is rapidly building to its climax. What is gained by having him at the Friar's cell when Juliet arrives (she could have easily told the Friar about the marriage plans)? How does he take her blunt responses to his overtures? How does the audience take them? What attitudes would you want to convey if you were playing her part here and, later, with the Friar? What convinces you that she means what she says to both men?
2. As with so many actions in this play, the Friar's suggestion seems not only eerie but foolhardy if one examines it carefully. Why take such chances if it's really no problem to get out

of Verona to Mantua, as the Friar plans to have Romeo and Juliet do when she awakens? (As earlier, why not simply tell Paris the truth?)

[*IV ii and iii*]

1. It's helpful to keep in mind that Juliet must play the dissembler once she knows that not even the Nurse is on her side any longer. In effect, she's alone, and she has multiple lies to tell and fearful acts to perform. What suggestions would you make to an actress playing Juliet about how to handle her lines and her outward actions in Scenes ii and iii? (Note that she makes no comment on hearing of the change in wedding date. It obviously can't be a matter of no importance to her. How would you suggest that the player react to the news?)
2. Would you call the misgivings Juliet has before drinking the potion reasonable or unreasonable? In either case, what do they reveal about the quality of her resolve?

[*IV iv and v*]

1. In Shakespeare's theater, Juliet's bed would have been in constant view, curtains closed all through this scene. Why is it important, dramatically, for the modern producer to arrange things similarly?
2. What does Shakespeare gain from the outlandish variety of behaviors with which he has crowded this scene, bringing it intentionally close to farce: the silly bustling of old Capulet? the servants preparing for the wedding feast? the overblown wailing over the "dead" Juliet? the buffoonish bad taste of Peter and the musicians?

[*V i*]

1. How, particularly for the audience, is the "flattering truth" of Romeo's dream yet one more example of the bulging list of ironic portents that crowd the play?
2. Romeo's plain and almost businesslike response to Balthasar's "ill news" is a far cry from his overwrought behavior in the Friar's cell the last time we saw him. How do his words and thoughts in the rest of the scene put in a different light his opening comments?
3. Why do you suppose his playwright makes so much of the apothecary, as we see him through Romeo's accurate surmises about the man? Is there in Romeo's attitude toward the apothecary pity or contempt, or a little of both? How do his

final words (lines 83–89) give further insight into the changes that banishment has brought?

[*V ii*]

1. How, in a sense, is the almost ludicrous ill-luck of Friar John's detainment not only believable but dramatically right at this point?
2. How do Laurence's words and plans in lines 24–30 reveal him finally for the shallow, sententious optimist he is and point up his human failings as being as dangerous in their way as Mercutio's and the Nurse's have been in theirs? In what sense may his be the most dangerous?

[*V iiii*]

1. This last is a long scene, and for those who like to indulge themselves, its mounting misery can be long drawn out. But that's not the way Shakespeare meant it to be handled, as the number of entrances and exists clearly suggests. If you were directing, how would you assure a sense of urgency in the progression of the scene without having it look like a Keystone Cops whirligig? Spell out in some detail how you would handle the goings and comings on the outer stage, how you would direct the actions in the tomb itself, where you would place the bodies of Romeo and Juliet at the end. (In Shakespeare's theater the tomb would have been in the inner playing area upstage, and Juliet on her slab would have been in full view all the while once the tomb is forced open.)
2. How do Paris's feelings about Juliet here (including his reasons for being at the tomb at all), coupled with what we've seen of him previously, bring Romeo's love for Juliet into sharp focus? Romeo calls him "gentle youth" and "boy." In what ways do those terms now fit Paris perfectly and Romeo not at all?
3. Show how all that happens in this scene, particularly the series of "ill-lucks" and "ill-doings" that bring on the final blood-lettings, is dramatically inevitable—that it has been carefully prepared for so that any last-minute deliverance would be absurd.
4. How might the pledges of Montague and Capulet to raise statues "in pure gold" in memory of their children—"poor sacrifices to our enmity"—be seen as the crowning irony of the play? Even though the lovers' deaths "bury their parents' strife," as the Prologue promises, how much have the living learned, judging by what is said and done at the end of the play?

SHAKESPEARE AND HIS WORKS

William Shakespeare was born in the Warwickshire town of Stratford on April 23, 1564 (a guess based on the record of his baptism dated April 26) and died there on April 23, 1616. He was the eldest of six children of John and Mary (Arden) Shakespeare. His father was a successful glovemaker and trader in Stratford and for a time was active in local civic and political affairs, serving for a term as high bailiff, or chief administrative officer of the town; his mother was the daughter of a prosperous landowner. At age 18 he married Anne Hathaway, a woman some eight years his senior. They had three children, Susanne in 1583, Hamnet and Judith (twins) in 1585.

Although he obviously spent most of his time in London between 1585 and 1611, he kept close ties with his home town, and his own family lived there throughout most of the year. In 1597 he purchased New Place, one of Stratford's finest homes, to which he retired in 1611.

There is no record of his formal schooling, but he undoubtedly attended the Stratford grammar school and got a solid grounding in Latin and literature since the masters during his school age years were Oxford graduates. When or why he went to London and turned to acting and writing plays is not known, but by 1592 he had clearly established a reputation in both fields; and for the next twenty years he turned out an average of almost two plays a year, plus a number of sonnets and several longer poems. He was a charter member of the Lord Chamberlain's Men, an acting company formed in 1594 (renamed the King's Men in 1603), the foremost company of its time. He remained with the King's Men until his retirement. In 1599 the company moved into the newly built Globe Theater, in which Shakespeare had a financial interest. By that time, and for the rest of his life, he prospered financially through his acting-writing-investing ventures. More important, in his own time he was a widely respected and widely loved dramatist in an age that produced many and for an audience that understood and supported the theater.

ii

A chronological listing of Shakespeare's published works follows. There is no certainty about most of the assigned dates, and probably never will be. As we have indicated in the Textual Note, there was in Shakespeare's day little of the concern we have for the printing of play scripts, and most of the assigned dates for composition are the result of scholarly research and supposition based on both external and internal evidence that we here need only to recognize.

PLAYS

1588–93	*The Comedy of Errors*
1588–94	*Love's Labor's Lost*
1590–91	*2 Henry VI*
1590–91	*3 Henry VI*
1591–92	*1 Henry VI*
1592–93	*Richard III*
1592–94	*Titus Andronicus*
1593–94	*The Taming of the Shrew*
1593–95	*The Two Gentlemen of Verona*
1594–96	*Romeo and Juliet*
1595	*Richard II*
1594–96	*A Midsummer Night's Dream*
1596–97	*King John*
1596–97	*The Merchant of Venice*
1597	*1 Henry IV*
1597–98	*2 Henry IV*
1598–1600	*Much Ado About Nothing*
1598–99	*Henry V*
1599	*Julius Caesar*
1599–1600	*As You Like It*
1599–1600	*Twelfth Night*
1600–1601	*Hamlet*
1597–1601	*The Merry Wives of Windsor*
1601–2	*Troilus and Cressida*
1602–4	*All's Well That Ends Well*
1603–4	*Othello*

1604	*Measure for Measure*
1605–6	*King Lear*
1605–6	*Macbeth*
1606–7	*Antony and Cleopatra*
1605–8	*Timon of Athens*
1607–9	*Coriolanus*
1608–9	*Pericles*
1609–10	*Cymbeline*
1610–11	*The Winter's Tale*
1611	*The Tempest*
1612–13	*Henry VIII*

POEMS

1592	*Venus and Adonis*
1593–94	*The Rape of Lucrece*
1593–1600	*Sonnets*
1600–1601	*The Phoenix and the Turtle*

Books, Records, Films

Further reading about Shakespeare's times, his theater, and the plays themselves is always valuable and enlightening. Suggested below is a short list of excellent books, most of which are in print in inexpensive editions. Also included is information about available recordings of the complete text of *Romeo and Juliet* and about films available on video, for rental or purchase.

Books

Books marked with an asterisk are available in inexpensive editions.

* Bentley, Gerald E. *Shakespeare: A Biographical Handbook.* New Haven: Yale University Press.

* Bradley, A. C. *Shakespearean Tragedy.* New York: Meridian Books.

Campbell, O. J., and Edward G. Quinn. *The Reader's Encyclopedia of Shakespeare.* New York: Thomas Y. Crowell.

Chambers, E. K. *William Shakespeare: A Study of Facts and Problems.* 2 vols. London: Oxford University Press.

* Dean, Leonard F. (ed.). *Shakespeare: Modern Essays in Criticism.* New York: Oxford University Press.

* Granville-Barker, Harley. *Prefaces to Shakespeare.* Vol. I. Princeton: Princeton University Press.

* Harbage, Alfred. *Shakespeare's Audience.* New York: Columbia University Press.

* Kernan, Alvin B. (ed.). *Modern Shakespearean Criticism.* New York: Harcourt Brace Jovanovich, Inc.

* Nagler, A. M. *Shakespeare's Stage.* tr. by Ralph Manheim. New Haven: Yale University Press.

Video

1954
Laurence Harvey, Susan Shentall, John Gielgud
138 minutes
Beta, VHS
Nelson Entertainment
Learning Corporation of America

1968
Directed by Franco Zeffirelli
Olivia Hussy, Leonard Whiting, Michael York, Milo O'Shea
138 minutes
Beta, VHS
Paramount Home Video

1979
BBC SHAKESPEARE SERIES
John Gielgud, Rebecca Saire, Patrick Ryecart
167 minutes
VHS
Time Life Video

1987
120 minutes
Beta, VHS
Films for the Humanities

Audio Recordings

All recordings are released in both monaural and stereo; the text will differ in minor respects from that used in this edition.

Caedmon
Claire Bloom, Albert Finney
3 cassettes
LC 67-566

Listen Pleasure
Alan Badel, Claire Bloom
2 cassettes
ISBN 0-88646-050-6